CAREER PLANNING FOR TEENS

How to Get Ahead, Plan for Your Dream Job, and Create a Bright Future

Charlie Haven

TABLE OF CONTENTS

INTRODUCTION **1**

CHAPTER 1: DISCOVERING YOURSELF **5**

Identifying Your Passions 6
Assessing Your Strengths 8
Understanding Your Personality Type 10
Your Values and Career Choice 12
Making Decisions 14
Key Takeaways 15
Online Resources 16

CHAPTER 2: THE WORLD OF WORK TODAY **17**

Navigating the Digital Job Landscape 18
The Gig Economy and Freelancing 21
Globalization and Remote Work 24
Technology's Impact on Traditional Roles 25
Key Takeaways 28
Online Resources 29

CHAPTER 3: MAPPING YOUR CAREER PATH **31**

Setting Career Goals 32
Exploring Career Pathways 35
The Role of Education in Your Career Path 38
Building a Career Action Plan 40
Key Takeaways 43
Online Resources 44

CHAPTER 4: DEVELOPING KEY SKILLS FOR SUCCESS **45**

Critical Thinking and Problem-Solving 46
Communication Skills for the Workplace 49
Teamwork and Collaboration 52
Leadership Skills for Future Leaders 55
Key Takeaways 59

CHAPTER 5: GAINING REAL-WORLD EXPERIENCE **61**

Internships: Gateway to Industry Experience 62
Volunteering 65
Part-Time Jobs: Learning on the Job 67

Summer Jobs 70
Key Takeaways 73
Online Resources 74

CHAPTER 6: NETWORKING AND MENTORSHIP 75

The Basics of Professional Networking 76
Mentorship 80
Using Social Media for Networking 83
Attending Industry Conferences and Workshops 87
Key Takeaways 90
Online Resources 91

CHAPTER 7: THE ART OF THE SIDE HUSTLE 93

Identifying Your Entrepreneurial Interests 94
The Basics of Starting a Side Hustle 97
Building a Brand on Social Media 100
Balancing School and Entrepreneurship 101
Key Takeaways 103

CHAPTER 8: PREPARING FOR THE JOB MARKET 105

Crafting a Standout Resume 106
The Art of Writing Cover Letters 109
An Effective Job Searching Strategy 111
Preparing for Job Interviews 112
Key Takeaways 116
Online Resources 117

CHAPTER 9: FACING FAILURE AND BUILDING RESILIENCE 119

Understanding Failure as a Learning Tool 120
Building Resilience 122
The Power of a Growth Mindset 124
Handling Rejection With Grace 126
Key Takeaways 128

CHAPTER 10: YOUR FUTURE STARTS NOW! 131

Taking the First Step 132
Continuous Learning and Skill Development 133
Documenting Your Journey 135
Key Takeaways 136
Online Resources 137

CONCLUSION 139

REFERENCES 143

Image References 157

INTRODUCTION

WHAT DO YOU WANT TO BE ONE DAY? YOU'VE NO doubt been asked this question many times. You might have answered very broadly by saying you want to be a fireman, a veterinarian, or a chef, for example. However, as you grow up and deal with the complexities of the world, the more you're forced to think about this question. Your hopeful career is no longer far in the future, but something you need to prepare for and make a reality through informed decisions. This can be a scary and intimidating thought because any choice you make about your career is life-changing. Know that you're not the only one feeling this way! In fact, surveys have found that about three-fourths of American teens were not fully confident in their career and college choices after graduation (Arundel, 2022).

Life is a learning process and it's okay that you might struggle in determining your career path or in figuring out what you want your future to look like. There are so many options that you can become overwhelmed, confused and get stuck. Alternatively, with some personal work and an informed plan, you can make decisions that motivate you to pursue a career that fits your personality, interests, and life goals.

When you use all the tools available to you, you can ensure a bright future. It's never too early to begin, and your teenage years are a great time to experiment and discover who you really are. Too often teens think that they have to wait until graduation to start preparing for their future. This thinking is flawed! There are so many opportunities you can grasp with both hands; opportunities that develop your skill set and give you valuable job experience.

Modern teens are among the luckiest in history because you have so many options and career avenues at your disposal. The contemporary world of work is like never before and requires personal innovation and determination. When you're truly passionate about something, you can mold your future to suit your needs and desires! That is what this book is for. In this guide, you will go on a journey of self-discovery and explore potential career paths that are right for you. By identifying your passions and interests, you'll find how they relate to the world of work today, and how you can best prepare for your career of choice. You will learn how to explore different career pathways and practice how to set goals that correspond with your unique vision of a bright future.

In this book, you'll learn how to develop your skills and find ways in which you can use these to advance your career. You'll learn how to enhance your communication, teamwork, and critical thinking skills—among others. You'll be encouraged to gain experience by perhaps starting an internship, getting a part-time job, or volunteering for an organization meaningful to you. You'll learn how to use networking and mentorship to your advantage and develop ways to apply these lessons to your career preparation. Maybe you want to start a side hustle for an extra income, something you'll learn how to do in this book too! You will also discover how to create an impressive resume and cover letter, navigate job-searching platforms, and much more!

Every chapter gives you practical tips to start constructing a future career you can be proud of. At the end of selected chapters, you'll find online resources that maximize your learning and encourage you to apply what you've been taught in the text. When you have this book handy, you can let go of your anxieties about the future. As you go through it and incorporate all its teachings into your plan, you will construct the amazing future you deserve. So, let's go on the exciting adventure of career planning!

CHAPTER 1:

Discovering Yourself

Knowing yourself is the beginning of all wisdom. –Aristotle

WHO ARE YOU? WHEN FACED WITH THIS QUESTION, you might be inclined to think about your name, how old you are, and where you go to school. Although these answers certainly form part of who you are, it's necessary to dig deeper. When you become aware of your unique strengths, interests, and values, you will be one step closer to unearthing your true self. Like everything else in life, finding out who you are and what makes you tick is a journey of discovery. Knowing all these things about yourself lays the foundation for who you want to be in the future and encourages you to engage in activities that bring your possible career purpose into clearer view. Sure, thinking about what job you want in the future might be daunting, but as you delve into the topics of this chapter, you'll be on the right path. Let's discover who you are!

Identifying Your Passions

Identifying your passions is a big leap toward knowing yourself. Passions guide you and can be great tools to indicate what you'll be good at in your career. A renowned American psychologist, Susan Newman, defines a *passion* as "an interest or activity that you can't get enough of; it keeps you coming back for more. It makes you inquisitive" (Proe, 2017). In other words, it's something that you do or think about quite often. This looks different for everyone. For example, you might enjoy working with numbers, whereas your friend enjoys playing a specific sport. The key is to find the deeper meaning of the activity and what draws you to it. If your favorite activity at school is to spend time with friends, you could read that as having great interpersonal skills with a subsequent passion for communication! Finding what your passions are can be done in three different ways.

Reflect

The first is to reflect on current activities that you enjoy. Simply put, what are some things you like doing? It's best to focus on things that don't seem like work to you because you choose to do them. Take some time to sit back and create a mental list of four things that you like doing. Once you have your list, think about why you feel fully absorbed and fulfilled by them. Answer questions like, do I feel good about myself when I do them? What do these activities have in common? And what does enjoying them teach me about myself? You'll soon find that all the activities you like have something in common. For instance, if you enjoy gardening and going on hikes, they both focus on being immersed in nature. By analyzing all the occasions where you felt the happiest, you'll come to know what it is you're passionate about. Note that when thinking of these times, don't focus on the attitudes and actions of others. Only you matter in finding your passions.

Broaden

The second way is to broaden your horizons. Of course, you enjoy specific things, but you might have hidden passions not yet explored! The only way to discover these is to try various kinds of activities. It's even better if it takes you out of your comfort zone because you'll learn things about yourself in the process. Doing something different will either prove that it's not for you or that it is. When doing something new, constantly remind yourself that there are no strings attached, and you don't have to do it again. Maybe it's a horrible experience, but it will have confirmed that the activity is not your passion. You can only know what you truly want when going through a period of trial and error. So, try something new and find out if you have a distinct passion yearning to get out.

Free Time

The third way is to take part in activities in your free time. All teenagers are expected to do specific things at school that could indicate passions but it's your responsibility to find other activities you enjoy. Your academic obligations are important, yet it's helpful to use some of your free time to look for additional interests. By investigating different kinds of hobbies and interests you take part in outside of school, you'll learn what you enjoy and advance in new skills. When trying different things, it's best to zone in on two or three after you've realized you like them. For example, if you like cooking, you could sign up for cooking classes at a community center and spend a lot of your free time doing that. You can then become an active participant and build yourself in a field of your choosing. The more you cultivate these experiences, the more you'll find a pattern that shows you your passions. Always ask yourself if you're enjoying the activity you're busy with and link it to your feelings on other occasions. Compare instances of fulfillment with instances of boredom, and you'll quickly find what your passions are!

Assessing Your Strengths

Everyone possesses several attributes that make them unique. You surely know that there is no one else on earth who looks like you. However, your differences on the inside are just as clear. You have a distinct set of strengths that you can work on further to excel in a career. In many cases, people are unaware of the strengths they have and need to be reminded so that they can grow them. When properly identified and advanced, your strengths will guide you toward a career that fits you.

One of the best ways you can find what your strengths are is by asking friends and family. Your loved ones know you the best and do not focus on your insecurities as much as you! They will be able to tell you what they think you're good at and may even offer you some advice on what you can do to become even better. Ask your loved ones questions like: What are my strengths? What do you admire about me? And what are you most likely to ask of me? When gathering all of these answers, you'll find a pattern of your strengths. For example, your parents might tell you that you're always helpful and make strangers feel welcome, allowing you to realize that one of your strengths is helping others. By recalling all their compliments after a specific action, your talents will become clearer.

That being said, you can also look for your strengths without the help of others. By simply looking at your everyday life, you can look for what you're good at. Of course, this involves analyzing all the compliments you get, but you can also look at your life objectively and see how your interests are acted upon. This means that you look at how you respond to your interests and how well you're able to do activities based on them. For instance, if you enjoy building small objects in your free time, you should look at how good the final product is and compare it with those made by people who share the same hobby. Perhaps you discover that you're better at it and that this is your unique strength!

People are naturally drawn to activities that they know they'll succeed in because no one likes failure. By taking your interests into account and how fulfilled you feel after doing a certain task associated with it, you'll see that your accomplishment is a personal strength. As you come to know what your strengths are, you're in the best position to look into careers that align with them and are naturally more prone to success.

Free Strength and Assessment Tools

You don't only have to trust yourself and your loved ones to discover your strengths. There are a variety of tools at your disposal. You can visit a career counselor when you're considering entering the job market. These are licensed professionals who are trained to conduct skills assessments and help you find what you'll be most effective at. If you don't want to do that just yet, you can look for free assessments online. A prominent one is called the Values in Action (VIA) Inventory of Strengths, first developed in 2004. This is a character assessment that asks you several questions about yourself and then uses your answers to give you a full analysis of all your personal strengths. You can find this online and receive a report on what you're good at, which can then be applied to various jobs you are most likely to thrive in. Another option is the Truity Career Personality Profiler, which operates similarly to VIA. Not only will this free online assessment display your strengths, but it will match them to your top career options. So, do some research and fill out a survey that will give a glimpse into your strengths!

Understanding Your Personality Type

Unlike passions and strengths, your personality refers to who you are at your core. It includes all your characteristics, such as being outgoing, kind, and responsible. There are too many personality traits to count, but when several traits are joined together, they usually form a personality type. You are undoubtedly very complex, and you probably already know what kind of person you are. Nevertheless, knowing your personality type carries many benefits for personal and professional growth.

A significant benefit is that it helps you identify your possible reactions. For example, if you know that you are more prone to acting on a feeling as opposed to a thought-out decision, you can prepare for an event beforehand. You know what situations are ideal for you because you recognize where you can trust yourself and what activities or experiences you feel uncomfortable with. Knowing your personality type also helps you to understand others and how you differ from them. When these differences are known, you can identify where you're more likely to prosper and surpass someone else. In other words, it gives you confidence in your abilities because you can sense what you'll be successful at. This is very important when thinking about your possible career.

Every career is best suited to a certain personality. By using the example of an extrovert and introvert, you'll find how crucial your personality type is. An extrovert is someone who gets their energy and drive from interacting with other people. As a result, they generate better work in team settings and feel fulfilled by these relationships. An introvert refers to a person who frequently finds it draining to interact with others and is very happy to work on their own without unnecessary communication. Extroverts are, therefore, more comfortable in jobs such as sales and public relations. It's no problem for them to approach strangers and strike up conversations with anyone! An introvert, on the other hand, is more likely to succeed in a field like writing or computer science because they're not expected to surround themselves with many people and constant communication.

Your personality type is essential in team dynamics. Almost every job needs some kind of collaboration between employees and between one's superior, like a manager. Self-awareness regarding your personality permits you to plan how you're going to interact with them and meet the goals of your organization or company. For instance, if you know you're an introvert, you can write down and memorize a few sentences that you want to say in a meeting.

There are no downsides to knowing your personality type. It gives you a glimpse into what job suits you and how you will act when employed. Remember, when there is a discrepancy between your personality and your career, it's much more difficult to find fulfillment and satisfaction!

Free Personality Assessment Tools

Just as you can find out about your strengths with online surveys, so can you learn about your personality type. Before taking a test, it's essential to remember that a survey can't give you all the information about yourself. You're too multifaceted for even the most intricate test to describe. However, personality quizzes can give you direction and the basic traits of who you are.

There are a variety of free online personality tests you can take, but two of these prove to be among the most reliable. The first is the 16Personalities test. Also called the Myers-Briggs Type Indicator (MBTI), the 16Personalities test is a questionnaire that indicates your primary traits. It does this by classifying binary values to opposite traits and finding where you fall on the scale. Once completed, you will be sorted into one of the 16 personalities and will be able to see what types of jobs are best suited for you. The second is the Big Five personality test. The test operates on the belief that there are five primary personality indicators—openness, conscientiousness, extroversion, agreeableness, and neuroticism. You will be placed on a scale regarding all of these and receive a result that will explain the findings. These tests are great tools to know what kind of person you are, and what career will suit you well.

Your Values and Career Choice

Values are defined as, "Basic and fundamental beliefs that guide your or motivate attitudes and actions" (Mintz, 2018). Your values help you recognize what is right or wrong behavior. Think about a time when you felt uncomfortable and conflicted. This was most likely an occasion where the situation was not in line with your values! You are led by core values that may include elements like honesty, creativity, courage, and compassion. Only you can identify what your values are, but there are some questions that can help you recognize them easier. Answer the following questions in your mind or on a piece of paper:

1. What was a meaningful moment in my life? What values were exemplified during this incident?
2. What was something that made me angry in the past week? What value was crossed here?

3. Who is one person I look up to? What values do they demonstrate?
4. What are two things that make me very angry? What values are absent when these happen?
5. What is my ideal work environment? What values do all the employees share?

Did your answers give you some clues about what you feel are your values? When you're in a career that goes against your values, you'll struggle to be as successful as you want to be. For example, if one of your values is a desire to try new things, working in a corporate setting with many layers of formal decision-making might not be for you. A company built on a strict bureaucratic system would understandably be very frustrating if you want to try out new ideas! This is why it's so important to research what the values of a company are before applying.

When you find a career closely aligned with your values, you will work with other people who are like you. For instance, if one of your values is kindness toward animals and you choose to go into the veterinary field, you'll be working with others who share this belief. Working in the confines of your values is, therefore, crucial because it makes you more motivated to progress in your career. All these aspects then lead to greater confidence and well-being because you'll feel like you're making a difference. When choosing between possible careers, it's advisable to look at the leading companies offering jobs in your respective field and note what their organizational values are. You should then compare them to your core values and see if they match up. If you find that they do, you're on the right track!

Making Decisions

Career planning while discovering yourself is all about decision-making. American entrepreneur Jim Rohn said, "You cannot make progress without making decisions" (Sutton, 2012). Decisions lie at the core of your entire life, and your future career depends on the choices you make as a teenager. Even though decisions are viewed as choosing one option over the other, it's a bit more intricate than that.

Jeff Bezos, the billionaire founder of Amazon, introduced a new way of looking at decisions. He distinguished between Type 1 and Type 2 decisions. Type 1 decisions are identified as "one way," meaning they're crucial decisions that have the ability to change your life. Moreover, though not impossible, they're not easily reversible. Choosing to move to another country, deciding on what your college major will be, and buying or selling a house fall into this category. Thought and consideration are keystones in these types of decisions because you have to be sure that they're right for you and that they add to the path you want your life to take. On the other side of the coin are Type 2 decisions. These decisions have less impact on your life and you can reverse them easily. They don't usually need a lot of thought and following your gut is oftentimes encouraged. You can merely make the decision and jump in!

In describing these types, Bezos advised his Amazon employees to remain mindful of whether a decision is Type 1 or Type 2. You wouldn't want to make a Type 1 decision on a whim! Because the stakes are higher for Type 1, you need to take your time and be deliberate. If you realize you're facing a Type 2 decision, then you can try it and take the risk. Bezos argues that people are prone to treating all decisions as Type 1 and sadly miss out on gaining valuable experiences by trying different things. You don't have to miss out on new experiences and learning curves when trying out several Type 2 options. The good news? Teens are in the best position to make many of these Type 2 choices! You have countless opportunities to make low-risk, easily reversible decisions before a Type 1 comes knocking at your door. You can fill your days with new experiences and learn different skills that will inform bigger decisions when the time comes.

So, take on new hobbies, take personality and strength quizzes, and get to know yourself now so that you're in the best position possible to know what you want. You are bound to make the correct decisions when you apply what you've learned about yourself in this chapter. Only then will you be prepared for the career that's right for you.

Now that you're closer to knowing who you are, we can move on. In the next chapter, we're going to be discussing the world of work today. The career options are like never before!

Key Takeaways

- To find the career best suited for you, you should discover who you are. Identifying your passions is the first step. This is done through self-reflection, broadening your exploration of different passions, and taking note of what you do in your free time.
- Finding your strengths is also important. Your friends and family can give you guidance about this, but you can also take a deep look at your interests and hobbies through personal reflection. Online assessment tools like the Values in Action (VIA) Inventory of Strengths are also available.
- Everyone has a unique personality. Your personality type dictates what career you'll thrive in. For example, the jobs best suited for extroverts are starkly different from those best suited

for introverts. You can learn more about your personality type by doing the 16Personalities test and the Big Five personality test.

- Your values play a big role in forming your career path. Your basic and fundamental beliefs should align with your career. For instance, if one of your values is service to others, a job in the medical field is more likely to provide personal and professional fulfillment.
- Your career path is based on the decisions you make. The founder of Amazon, Jeff Bezos, introduced the idea of Type 1 and Type 2 decisions. Type 1 decisions are life-changing choices that aren't easily reversible. Type 2 decisions are smaller, easily reversible decisions that you can risk trying. As a teen, many of your decisions fall into the Type 2 category, so go for it! Jump in and try something new!

Online Resources

- **Big 5 Personality Test:** https://my-personality-test.com/big-5
- **16Personalities Test:** https://www.16personalities.com/
- **Truity Career Personality Profiler:** https://www.truity.com/
- **Values in Action (VIA) Inventory of Strengths:** https://www.viacharacter.org/

CHAPTER 2:

The World of Work Today

Let us realize that: the privilege of work is a gift, the power to work is a blessing, the love of work is success! –David O. McKay

THE MODERN WORLD OF WORK IS STARKLY DIFFERENT from 20 or even 10 years ago. The rapid rate at which new technologies develop creates jobs, changes current ones, and expands career possibilities. In fact, research has found that once-thriving American industries in the 1950s—such as rubber manufacturing—have decreased to a fraction of their original sizes in the 21st century (Kiersz, 2019). In its place are new jobs like social media managers, smartphone developers, and various posts in the renewable energy sector. Some even argue that in the next few years, entirely new industries will be created with endless job openings. This is not something you need to be afraid of. Rather, you can be excited about the many opportunities you will have as you advance in your career!

It's safe to say that traditional career paths are ever-changing. When you learn how to account for these in choosing a career and finding eventual employment, you'll be more successful than you think possible. Let's discover how you can navigate the digital job landscape!

Navigating the Digital Job Landscape

It's no secret that we're living in the digital age. Everywhere you look you see machines, smartphones, and computers. You even need to type on a touchscreen when you order at your favorite fast-food restaurant! Careers in the digital age are all built on several broad professional skills. Five of these can be highlighted.

The first is emotional intelligence. Even though this was a skill needed in many historical jobs as well, emotional intelligence is crucial to the increasingly complex nature of modern jobs. Simply put, complex work requires complex collaboration between employees. For example, when working on a new app, the creators need to be true team players and use their communal strengths to fulfill their tasks.

The second is having a "geek acumen." Being a "nerd" is not only something to be proud of but will actively assist you in performing modern jobs. Learning skills in the area of coding or computer science will help you in jobs that aren't even solely based on this. If you're a doctor, you will still need to use complex machinery in the surgery room!

The third is virtual collaboration. The days of doing your job in the absence of technology are over, because practically all employees have to communicate via email or online meetings that they have to operate appropriately.

The fourth is critical problem-solving. Of course, problem-solving is crucial to many different careers. However, the uncertainty regarding future careers requires you to have the basics prepared. You can't expect to know what jobs will be in demand; you don't have control over that. Yet, when you have problem-solving skills in the bag, you'll be able to adapt to any work-related situation that comes your way. In past careers, problem-solving followed a linear process whereby the issue was identified, and data was collected to find a solution. In the modern workforce, you'll have to take note of various problems and think of more comprehensive ways to solve them. This might be more work but it's definitely more rewarding!

Lastly, you should have the skill of cultural intelligence. Accompanying the digital age is cultural globalization. This means that different kinds of people all over the world work together and everyone deserves respect. In the past, most people stayed in their communities with their colleagues often being their neighbors as well! This is no longer the case. You need to practice cross-cultural empathy and embrace the differences of others by communicating effectively with a very diverse workforce.

Digital Platforms as Career Launchpads

Finding work is digital as well. Speak to most young adults and you'll find that practically all of them applied to their current jobs online! All modern companies publicize openings on platforms that are frequented daily by job seekers. Very few of them still list vacancies in the newspaper and prefer to upload a post on career websites. This widens their target market but also means that you'll need to stand out because they have many prospective employees to choose from.

Perhaps the most famous digital platform for advertising and finding work is LinkedIn. Analysis of the platform has found that about 140 job applications are submitted on LinkedIn every second (Macready, 2024)! Another well-known website is Indeed. This platform works similarly to LinkedIn and claims that they have about 350 million job seekers visiting the website all over the world (*Our Company*, n.d.).

Other platforms, such as Upwork, are also visited by freelance workers who want to connect with employers offering jobs that don't necessarily include a yearly contract. All of these websites can launch a prosperous career because they allow you to showcase your skills, connect you with employers, and give you the ability to find work opportunities globally. These platforms rely only on your ability for self-branding, a relatively new concept.

Self-Branding

Self-branding is defined as the "practice of establishing a positive public perception of a person by showcasing their positive traits" (Khalid, 2022). It means that you put in the work to look appealing to prospective employers by standing out from the crowd. The ability to stand out is a major element in landing the job that you want because online competition is oftentimes fierce. Luckily, there are a variety of tools you can use to your advantage. When the time comes that you're ready to enter the job market, there are four things you need to remember.

1. **Perfect your online presence.** Your online presence refers to a publication of your professional identity. You should have a professional photograph and a record of your skills and possible experience on all the job market platforms you choose to subscribe to. Your goal is to create a robust online profile that keeps prospective employers intrigued.

2. **Use various online platforms.** Your profile should optimally be published on various websites such as those discussed above. The more platforms you subscribe to, the better your chances are of landing a job of your choice.

3. **Customize.** Many job seekers make the mistake of sending the same resume and cover letter to all the companies they apply to. This is not recommended! Before applying for a job on one of these platforms, do some research about the company by visiting its official website. Learn what their values are, what they want in an employee, and what their guiding principles are. When you know these, you can tweak your resume to fit their mold.

4. **Network.** You are likely to succeed if you apply to a variety of job postings, however, you're more likely to land the job of your choice if you become involved in the online marketplace. Many employment platforms like LinkedIn have forums and professional groups that anyone can join. When you join one of these, you come across as proactive and might make an impression on a certain company. For example, when a company hosts a virtual event, take your chance and join them. Who knows? Maybe you can talk to a recruiter!

The Gig Economy and Freelancing

Something unique to our time is the gig economy. In the past, people would have a set number of hours, a monthly salary, and certain tasks that remained the same. Today, an increasing number of people find employment in short-term jobs or go at it themselves, known as freelancing. This new gig economy is growing, with about 36% of Americans in 2024 taking part in short-term work as their primary or secondary source of income (*Gig Economy Statistics,* 2024). The expanding number of gigs is surely promising, but this trend has led to questions regarding issues such as workers' rights and an employer's contractual obligations.

The main issue if you choose to become part of the gig economy is security versus flexibility. A traditional job usually offers you security with a constant payout and several benefits like health insurance and paid time off. Freelance workers, on the other hand, face irregular pay and mostly have to pay for their own personal benefits like a pension fund. By looking at several pros and cons of freelance work, you can get some clarity on deciding whether this is something you want to look into when you're ready.

A significant advantage is that you can choose to work where you want. Freelance work allows you to work wherever you may be. Some people travel while working! You can also choose when you work, meaning you can sleep late and adjust your work hours to times that fit your personal schedule. Another pro is that it's very affordable to start. In most cases, all you need is a computer and an internet connection. Add to that the high demand for independent contractors and many are drawn to the gig economy. You're also able to choose what clients you want to work with and can structure a work/life balance that works for you.

However, the primary drawback is that the work isn't always consistent. One month, you may be really busy, and the next, you can't find work! Without savings, this can be hazardous. Additionally, many freelancers have several customers with deadlines of their own. Without proper planning, you run the risk of being overworked and stressed. There are also more legal and financial responsibilities. Work contracts, taxes, and insurance will be on your shoulders and might push you toward looking for a financial adviser who expects a salary as well. Freelance work is, therefore, a highly individualistic endeavor that doesn't only involve a quick buck. It needs proper planning and legal awareness. Always make sure that you know the rules and regulations regarding freelancing in your area.

Becoming a Freelancer

Being a freelancer differs depending on what you want to do. However, there are some principles that will guide you in the majority of freelancing options. The most common method is to visit freelancer websites like Upwork and Freelancer.com. This will give you a general idea of what is expected from you and what jobs are in demand. It will also indicate what the pay rates are for the specific niche that you fall in.

Once you've done this, it's time to come up with a game plan: You have to decide what services you'll be offering. You can either go for general opportunities or specialize in a certain field. For example, you can offer services in social media management on various social media platforms or publicize yourself as only managing on Instagram. While doing this, it's crucial that you identify your target market.

Ask yourself questions like: Who will hire me? What age group would be most interested in my services? And what are the professions of those who would want this service? When you understand these, you can work out a rate, if needed. You set a rate by looking at what other freelancers are asking for. If you see they ask $200 for managing a blog, for instance, you can offer $180. Clients will always look for a bargain!

All of your research can then guide you in creating an online portfolio that impresses potential customers. Here, you can use what you learned in the previous section about standing out among the crowd. It's also essential to market yourself. Luckily, you have the ability to make your own website, create profiles highlighting your services on social media, or send emails to potential customers on your freelancing platform. With a great profile and a little determination, anyone can quickly find their first gig!

Globalization and Remote Work

Although freelancing is something that is usually done from home, many established companies have started to offer remote positions as well. During the COVID-19 outbreak, the notion of working from home gained traction. Employers saw that their employees were just as effective from home as they were in the workplace. By 2023, about 35% of Americans worked remotely with no plans of going back to the office (Parker, 2023).

One can suspect why this trend is so popular among many companies. The main reasons are that they don't have to rent or purchase large offices, ensure parking, and offer day-to-day perks like coffee to their employees. Plainly put, it's cheaper to hire remote workers! Moreover, many employers promote remote work because it expands the talent pool of prospective workers. Most countries allow foreign nationals to be employed as foreign workers. A company can, therefore, hire someone from another country and doesn't have to think about relocating them to the company headquarters.

It's important to remember that not all jobs can be done from home, though. You wouldn't expect a builder to be a remote worker! Nonetheless, highly administrative jobs like financial services are increasingly being performed at home. This is a reality you will come to terms with when you enter the job market. There are several things you should consider before entering a job that permits this.

Working from home leads to greater isolation. Sure, some people are introverts, but communication and interaction are fundamental human needs. If you don't spend enough time with people in your personal life, remote work has been linked to a greater prevalence of mental health conditions like depression and stress (Platts et al., 2022).

Particularly when you're starting out in a career, working remotely can mean you miss out on getting to know colleagues, observing other more experienced people at work, and the informal "water cooler" type moments to catch up with others, which can be invaluable when you're establishing yourself in the workplace. There are also some remote workers who claim to struggle with overworking. As they don't leave their work at the office like they used to, they forget that their home should be a sanctuary of comfort and relaxation. When a special area of the home isn't designated as the primary "office," you may struggle to forget about your work responsibilities. This has also been shown to lead to disrupted sleep (Platts et al., 2022).

Remote work is also an expense in itself. You understandably use more electricity, internet, and drinks than you would if you went into the office. Nonetheless, remote working isn't going anywhere! New tools and technologies continue to be developed, which gives the impression that it's only growing further. Communication platforms like Zoom and Slack are used as collaboration tools between work teams. Project management platforms like Trello and Asana are also employed by remote teams every day. The diversity and innovation of remote work have only grown. You can expect to occasionally be at home if you become an office worker!

Technology's Impact on Traditional Roles

The modern workforce has also witnessed expanding automation. *Automation* is defined as "the creation and application of technologies to produce and deliver goods and services with minimal human intervention" (Rouse, 2023). Minimal human intervention scares many people because they argue that companies prefer cheaper machinery over employees who come with a range of demands. However, proponents claim that human intervention remains an important element of automation.

It's logical that unskilled labor will face layoffs, but this opens the door to better training and skill building. In fact, many companies that advance automation train their employees to work with new machinery and technologies rather than run automated systems. Research has found this to be true with some finding that automation is a driving force behind the creation of jobs (Harris, 2020). This increases overall productivity and stimulates the economy, which in turn leads to more job openings.

In sectors like healthcare, finance, and manufacturing, automation is a reality all job seekers need to come to terms with. Automation not only creates new jobs, but it also lessens the need for people to work in uncomfortable or even dangerous environments. For example, automation allows energy workers to refrain from heavy labor in the mining industry and spurs prospective employees to train in skills that will permit them to operate mining machinery.

Accompanying automation is *artificial intelligence (AI)*, which is defined as "the simulation of human intelligence processes by machines, especially computer systems" (Laskowski & Tucci, 2022). AI differs from automation because it involves more intricate technological programs capable of performing a variety of human functions. In recent years, AI has even been used in hospital operating rooms with robotic surgery gaining steam.

The topic of AI makes many people weary because they're afraid of what it would mean for unskilled workers. A survey conducted in the United States in 2022 found that about 37% of Americans are concerned about what it would mean for the future (Rainie et al., 2022). Although AI will lead to a drop in certain sectors, the promise of augmented AI is evident. This is a subset of AI that is designed to work with an employee, as opposed to replacing them. Hence, someone would work with the assistance of AI systems and be more productive as a result. This carries endless benefits for detail-oriented jobs and lessens the time required for data-heavy tasks. AI is still in its infancy and can be expensive and complex for companies to acquire, but it will quickly become mainstream so work on your skills in technology now to make sure you're prepared for however AI develops!

Upskilling and Reskilling

The earlier-mentioned example of learning to work with new automated systems is referred to as upskilling, a process that teaches existing workers to enhance their current work responsibilities. Companies frequently engage in upskilling as the workspace changes in the face of development. Reskilling, on the other hand, is more elaborate because it tasks an employee with learning a completely new set of skills that can help them perform a new job. Both of these are crucial to the modern workforce.

The rapid changes that companies encounter make upskilling and reskilling essential. It's likely that you'll access one or both of these when you enter the workforce. The key attributes that you should foster are adaptability and a love of learning. You wouldn't want to stay in the same position for your entire life–that would surely be boring! Try different things at school, meet new people, and foster a sense of wonder and excitement for the unknown. By working on these personal skills, you'll be in the best position to manage work-related changes favorably.

Now that you got a glimpse of the modern world of work, we can look at what you envision your career to be in the future. In the next chapter, you're going to map your career path!

Key Takeaways

- The modern world of work is completely different from that of the previous century. The most visible change is increasing digitalization. In this new technological age, employees need five broad skills: emotional intelligence, "geek acumen," virtual collaboration, problem-solving, and cultural intelligence.
- Finding work is digital, too. Online platforms like LinkedIn are extensively used by employers to publish job openings and by job seekers to find work. Therefore, the concept of self-branding is important for prospective applicants.
- In the modern age, the gig economy has become more prevalent. This describes short-term jobs, with many people choosing to become freelancers. The primary concern in the gig economy is flexibility versus stability. Becoming a freelancer places all the responsibility on you, with taxes—to name only one—falling solely on your shoulders.
- Increasing globalization has also led to changes. People from different countries and cultures are expected to work together. Contributing to this has been remote work whereby an increasing number of people are working from home. This has many advantages but can threaten mental health as employees become more socially isolated.
- The development of new technologies has led to automation in many economic sectors. Although some are concerned about

what this means for job seekers, automation can be used to teach workers new skills. AI has also gone mainstream with computers doing many jobs originally done by people. This can cause some job losses, but augmented AI makes many jobs more productive.

Online Resources

- **Freelancer.com:** https://www.freelancer.com/
- **Indeed:** https://www.indeed.com/
- **LinkedIn:** https://www.linkedin.com/
- **Upwork:** https://www.upwork.com/

CHAPTER 3:

Mapping Your Career Path

Find out what you like doing best and get someone to pay you for doing it. –
Katharine Whitehorn

EVERY CAREER PATH LOOKS DIFFERENT. IF YOU SPEAK to the adults in your life, you'll find that they all went on unique journeys that led them to where they are today. That being said, all of the successful stories have decision-making and planning in common. Oftentimes, the happiest adults are those who correctly matched their passions to career objectives and currently enjoy work they knew would be right for them. This is backed up by evidence.

One study found that people who are happy in their careers are 12% more productive than those who don't find fulfillment in their job tasks (Revesencio, 2015). You surely don't want a career that doesn't bring you fulfillment! The only way to avoid this is by preparing for your future career and knowing exactly what you want in a job. Because you're still young, you are probably not 100% sure of what you want to do. Don't worry, most people don't! However, when you do some research and personal work, you'll quickly start to find out what type of career will suit you best. Let's map your career path!

Setting Career Goals

In Chapter 1, you learned about finding your passions and your strengths. As a result, you're in a better position to start thinking about your optimal future. Before developing career goals, you'll need to envision what you want your life to look like. Envisioning your future self doesn't only mean that you think about the job you'll have. Instead, think about everything. Where do you want to live? Do you want to go on many trips? Do you want stability or greater employee flexibility? Do you want to work in an office full-time or do remote work?

By closing your eyes and creating a mental picture of what a typical Monday will look like in 10 years, you'll be able to construct an idea of what you want. There are several tips that can assist you in doing this. One is to think about your hobbies and values. Namely, what is important to you and what will bring you the most satisfaction. Also, consider what your talents are and what your ideal work environment is; these are important factors as well. Make sure to reflect on the type of people you want to surround yourself with and the impact you want to have in the world around you.

Perhaps one of the greatest tips is to think about what legacy you want to have. Simply put, what do you want people to remember about you regarding your career when you're no longer here? When you envision these future scenarios, you'll be closer to finding your career path. Once you have an idea, make it visual. Create a vision board with pictures of your life in 10 or 15 years. A vision board is a very powerful, motivating, and aspirational tool. When you create a visual image of what you want, it keeps you inspired and encourages you to make it real. Paste pictures of your future home, your family, your car, your office, and anything that uplifts you. The board doesn't have to be perfect; it can include various things that motivate you!

Nonetheless, make room for goal adaption. This refers to changing your goals in the face of new circumstances. For example, if you've already created a vision board and you've found a new hobby, don't be afraid to add it to your vision board. Flexibility is key and you should always make room for revising your goals as your personal interests change and the job market evolves. In other words, don't remain too set on one thing, but work on adding things to your goals to make them more comprehensive. A great way to do this is by scheduling a monthly check-in of your goals. Ask yourself whether they account for any changes you've gone through. How can the goals be made better? Have circumstances changed how I will realize these goals? And how can I stay on course? To do this, you should have clear, set goals to jump from. This is where the SMART guidelines come into play!

SMART Goals

SMART is an acronym that outlines certain principles for defining your goals. It can be used for anything, but it's especially effective when applied to your career objectives. You can use the SMART guidelines to work on preliminary career goals and add or modify them as you adapt your approaches. The great thing about SMART is that it can motivate you toward meeting certain career goals while leaving room for changes whenever you think necessary. SMART is defined as the following:

- **"S" refers to being specific.** When you describe your goal in as much detail as possible, you're more likely to succeed. Career goals should not be too broad. Sure, you can have the goal of being a financial accountant in the future, but your specific goal as a teen should be to prepare for this. For example, make the goal of signing up for a short online course in accounting that you do in your free time. Not only can you meet this goal in a timely manner, but it adds to your ultimate objective.

- **"M" refers to being measurable.** This means that you should keep track of the steps you're taking to meet the specific goal. If you want to go to college to study dentistry and you know that you need a certain grade in math, your goal could be to perform better academically. Being measurable in this context implies that you record your rising grades in texts and exams. This will keep you on track.
- **"A" refers to asking yourself whether your goal is achievable.** Some careers have certain restrictions and if you know you can't meet them—even with all possible efforts—you should change the career to one that suits your needs. Moreover, by breaking your bigger goals up into smaller ones, the likelihood of achievability increases. So, keep your vision on a broad goal, but create smaller, achievable goals that would slowly lead you there.
- **"R" refers to checking whether your goal is relevant.** All your shorter goals should play a part in reaching your ultimate goal. For example, if you want to be an English teacher, the goal of perfecting your sports skills isn't as crucial as practicing your writing abilities! When setting short-term goals, always ask yourself whether it will assist you in realizing your envisioned future.
- **"T" refers to the importance of time.** Finally, ending up in a career is still a ways off from being realized. When you set goals that help you meet that one, ensure that you set deadlines. If

you want to go into nursing and volunteer at a local nursing home, set a goal that you'll be working there for three months. This will add structure to your life and make you feel accomplished when finished. Always remember that your career pathway will be unique, and you don't have to compare yourself to anyone. Your career path is just as distinctive as your goals!

Exploring Career Pathways

Your career path doesn't have to be linear. In the past, people believed that you go to school, then study a course at college, and finally end up in a certain job for the rest of your life. As you've found, the modern world of work is far more complex! You are bound to take many unexpected turns on your road to a prosperous career. Many influential people took the nonlinear approach and made a success of their lives.

One of these is Jack Andraka who invented a revolutionary diagnostic tool to detect pancreatic cancer. He was still in high school and had no formal training in medicine but researched the topic in his free time. He would go on to win prestigious awards for his contributions to medicine and was already accomplished when he went to college! Jack proves that a career path can look unusual, and that personal experience is the most important element.

Yet, the nonlinear approach rests on three aspects. First, it involves an attitude of learning where you invest in your future by building experience through many activities. Second, it involves being open to different kinds of opportunities. By exploring various skills and avenues, you'll discover your interests. Third, it involves encouraging networking with successful people who live the life you aspire to.

Maybe you've heard the saying, "It's who you know, not what you know!" These are essential for the nonlinear path.

Whether you choose to follow a strictly linear path or not, the importance of internships and shadowing shouldn't be overlooked. Both of these activities give you the ability to operate in a work environment with no strings attached. They aren't usually prerequisites for admission to college, but they make you stand out in your application. By interning or shadowing in a field you find interesting, you'll see how it operates. It will either confirm that your career choice is correct or indicate that you should look into other options. You will learn from employees, network with bosses, and develop soft skills like interpersonal collaboration.

There are no downsides to immersing yourself in the environment you hope to work in one day! You don't have to wait for your school to offer internships. You can be proactive by doing your own research. You can either talk to family and friends about the possibility of shadowing. Maybe you can go directly to the company in question and ask them about opportunities for teens. As always, the internet is a great resource. Three websites that offer internships and shadowing opportunities are LinkedIn, Glassdoor, and Chegg Internships. Take some time to contact prospective employers via email or phone calls, and you'll be on the road to a possible work opportunity.

Career Clusters and Pathways

It may be daunting to pinpoint the exact job you want someday. Luckily, the concept of career clusters makes this easier. A *career cluster* is defined as, "a group of occupations with similar features" (*Career Cluster and Career Pathways*, n.d.). It, therefore, broadens your perspective by designating several jobs with related characteristics in certain groups.

The National Career Clusters Framework is used in the United States and identifies 16 clusters, with each one sharing many necessary skills, activities, and interests. Under these 16 clusters are 79 jobs! For example, the cluster known as "Government and Public Administration," details a variety of jobs dealing with issues like national security, taxation, and foreign service. When learning about these clusters, it'll be easier for you to make a decision because you know what your general interests and abilities are. By using the online resource marked "The National Career Clusters Framework" as your basis, you can take the following steps:

1. **The first step is to conduct a career interest inventory.** You surely know what you like, but taking a test will help you frame your interests more objectively. A great resource is the Holland Career Test. This survey operates by using six job areas and gives you a score in each after you've completed the questions. Make sure to read your results slowly and find where your highest score is.
2. **The second step is to match your results to a few clusters.** For example, if your highest score in the Holland test was for the investigative element, you can take a look at the cluster called "Science, Technology, Engineering and Mathematics." By researching this, you'll find several jobs in the cluster and may even discover what college courses are most popular in this group.
3. **The third step is to learn as much as you can about your cluster.** When you decide on a cluster, as opposed to a specific job, you have the benefit of making general decisions regarding what college major or experience you need. Ask yourself: What are some courses that will allow me to do a variety of jobs in this

cluster? And what pathway—such as going to college or not—works when looking for jobs in this cluster?

The Role of Education in Your Career Path

Decisions around going to college are very dependent on the job you want. Many high school students take going to college as a given, no matter what they want to do. This is not recommended. Before embarking on a college course, you need to be sure that it's what you really want and need.

There are several advantages and disadvantages of going to college. The primary advantage is that college opens you up to more career possibilities and a myriad of studies have found that college grads earn more than their counterparts (Evans, 2023). However, this is only because jobs in areas like finance require a completed four or three-year course for entry. If you want to go into carpentry, for example, going to college or not won't make a difference to your eventual salary!

Additional advantages are that you'll work on your personal and academic skills, as well as networking with others in your field of choice. On the flip side, college can be really expensive. Many former students spend years paying off student loans and struggle to get ahead with a chunk of their salary going to their debts. Most college courses are also very intensive, minimizing the time you have for a side job or gaining experience in your field of choice. Even so, going to college doesn't automatically lead to a job and you'll still need to apply to various positions before you land employment when your course is complete.

It is, therefore, very important that you look at what you want to do and investigate other options. There has been an increasing trend in online learning platforms and courses that don't cost as much while being certified. Moreover, your prospective job might benefit from you going to a trade or vocational school. Electricians, plumbers, pharmacy technicians, and masseurs all go to trade and vocational schools and, in some cases, earn more than those who went to college!

Jobs in technology, like computer programmers and web developers, can also be found with an online certificate from an accredited online institution. If you want to work in retail, you can start small and slowly build yourself up to senior roles. You might start off as a shop assistant, only to gain experience and end up managing the store in a year or two.

Whether you go to college or not, you should aspire to be a lifelong learner. This notion is especially critical if you don't have a degree. The more experience you gain and short courses you do in your free time, the more you build your portfolio and ensure a prosperous career. In summary, you have many options available to you and you should only make a decision when you've researched all the alternatives.

I Want to Go to College

If you decide to go to college, you have the responsibility of choosing a major. This is an important decision because it will guide your career path. To make the correct decision, you have to research all the majors in your cluster and think of how well they match up with your career goals. If you have an idea of the major you want to pick, ask yourself the six following questions:

1. Is the major general enough to be applied to various jobs in my cluster of choice?
2. Do I envision myself working in this field for 20 or 30 years?
3. When I finish my bachelor's degree, will I need to pursue a postgraduate degree to work in the field?

4. Are there many jobs in this field, and do they correlate to what I envision my salary to be?
5. Are there other majors that look appealing to me? Should I take a look at them before making a decision?
6. Is this major congruent with my personality, talents, and skills?

When you answer all of these questions honestly, you're putting yourself in the best position to make the right decision for your future. These questions can also be applied to courses in trade and vocational schools or online platforms. By analyzing your answers, you'll ensure that you're not wasting your time on a course that is not right for you. Pass this Type 1 decision through this test and you'll be on the right track!

Building a Career Action Plan

As you now know the basics of how to structure your career, it's time to actively set up your career plan. A *career plan* refers to "your professional goals and the steps [you take] to achieve them" (Shorelight Team, 2023). Before discussing the actionable steps, you need to remember a few things. Your plan is best broken up into smaller steps. This has been mentioned, but it begs repeating! The smaller your steps are, the more likely you are to achieve them. For example, your only goal can't be to one day be an engineer. Of course, this can be your ultimate goal, but your current goals should be more immediate and place you on a path that will ensure your engineering future.

Additionally, your career action plan must include the elements of flexibility and adaptability. It's certain that you'll meet some roadblocks or fail while trying to meet smaller goals. Don't be so focused on the end goal that you lose all motivation when a small step fails. There is always a way around it!

Lastly, your career action plan requires you to track your progress along the way. The plan is something you'll need to reevaluate and change as the circumstances do. Encourage feedback and be prepared to incorporate new things into the plan that ensure you stay aligned with your career expectations. With that said, let's learn how to create your plan!

The Four Easy Steps in Building a Career Plan

1. **Do a self-assessment.** It's only when you take a close look at yourself that you can know what kind of job will suit you. In Chapter 1, you learned how to identify your passions, strengths, talents, and personality type. Use all of the resources there to get clarity on what kind of person you are. Don't be overly critical of yourself but be realistic. If you're not that good at math, a job in rocket science might not be for you! It's best to write all of your personal findings on a piece of paper or in a document on your computer. That way, you'll see all your attributes clearly and how you'll come across to potential employers.

2. **Create a list of possible careers.** When you make use of the clusters and do a quiz like the Holland test, you can find where you fit in. After you've identified your cluster, do some research about all the jobs that fall under the banner. Learn what each job entails and match them up with the personal sheet you created in Step 1. Ask questions like, do I see myself working in one of these cluster jobs? Do I think that it'll enrich my life? And what difference will I be able to make when employed in this cluster?

3. **Narrow your cluster down into specific jobs.** There are numerous jobs in each cluster and most of them have starkly

different daily tasks. Some offer higher salaries or tend to recruit more staff. Prioritize the cluster you identified in Step 2, and measure how each one of these fits with your envisioned future. For example, do you want to work remotely or in an office? Are there opportunities for the job in your town or city, or are you willing to move far away should you have to? A great tool here is LinkedIn and the official websites of the companies offering certain jobs. Go through your list of potential cluster jobs and learn how the benefits and downfalls of each one fit in your hopeful future. When this is complete, narrow your choices down by identifying no more than three similar jobs you'll be good at.

4. **Start by setting your career goals and stick to them.** Because your three potential careers are in the same cluster, planning for them will be similar, too. The objective of this step is to place you in the best position possible to make one of these jobs a reality. Think about what small steps you need to take by setting SMART goals. It's best if your SMART goals don't have deadlines longer than six months because this will keep you motivated and encourage you to set new ones when they're complete. Relate your school subjects, volunteering opportunities, and ideas for job shadowing to your potential career. For example, if you want to go into architecture, search for afterschool programs or volunteering opportunities that offer training in design software. When you find one, set a SMART goal that is attainable. Should you complete this goal, set another one that gradually builds you up until you're ready to go to college or get training in your respective field. As a teenager, your career action plan doesn't have to be perfect! You might recall the differences between Type 1 and Type 2 decisions. Engage in as many Type 2 decisions as you can and stay dedicated to your

career action plan. Always adapt it if necessary and visit your plan as much as you can!

With a great career plan, you're bound to make your dream career a reality. However, to be even more effective, you'll need to work on your personal and professional skills. In the next chapter, you'll learn how to develop the key skills for success!

Key Takeaways

- Your career path is one of the most important decisions you'll ever make. Therefore, it needs a clear plan! When thinking of your career goals, you need to be flexible, and it's beneficial to create a vision board as a source of inspiration.
- When setting goals that will guide you toward your preferred career, it's best to break them up into smaller, actionable steps. Setting goals can be done by using the SMART system. SMART states that all your goals should be specific, measurable, achievable, relevant, and completed in a timely manner.
- Your career path will be unique. There are some that take the linear approach, but you may take a nonlinear approach. To succeed in a nonlinear path, you should have an attitude of learning, open yourself up to different opportunities like internships, and network with people in your desired field.
- You may not know the exact job you want. However, you probably know what field you want to work in. Namely, your career cluster. A career cluster refers to "a group of occupations with similar features" (*Career Cluster and Career Pathways*, n.d.). In the United States there are 16 clusters you

can choose from. You can identify your cluster by doing the Holland Test and finding what skills you're best at.

- Choosing to go to college or not is a life-changing decision. It shouldn't be done lightly and requires a lot of research. Before choosing to go to college, learn whether the field you want to go in needs a degree. Other education options include vocational or trading school and online certificates.
- Building your career action plan consists of four steps. First, do a self-assessment. Second, create a list of possible career niches using the clusters system. Third, narrow your cluster down into certain jobs. Last, set smaller career goals—like getting a certain grade for a specific school subject—and stick to them.

Online Resources

- **Chegg Internships:** https://www.chegg.com/
- **Glassdoor:** https://www.glassdoor.com/
- **Holland Career Test:** https://www.truity.com/test/holland-code-career-test
- **LinkedIn:** https://www.linkedin.com/
- **National Careers Clusters Framework:** https://www.asvabprogram.com/career-cluster

CHAPTER 4:

Developing Key Skills for Success

Nobody ever mastered any skill except through intensive persistent and intelligent practice. –Norman Vincent Peale

WHAT SKILLS DO YOU THINK ARE MOST IMPORTANT IN the modern workplace? You probably thought about things like cultural intelligence you read about earlier. This is a good starting point and helps you realize how critical some skills are in finding a career of your choice. *Skills* are generally defined as, "people's abilities, knowledge, and expertise that are needed to carry out specific tasks or activities effectively" (*What Are Skills?* n.d.).

All jobs are based on a range of personal and professional skills. That's why interviewers commonly ask you about yours! Of course, the required skills for certain jobs differ, but if you ensure you have several broad, all-encompassing skills, you'll be able to build on them and modify them to suit any job you want to do. This is not to say that specific skills should be ignored. A chef needs excellent culinary skills to work at the best restaurants, for example. Yet, there are a few skills that link all careers, and when you attain them, you're bound to perform optimally in any career. Let's see what these are and how you can develop them!

Critical Thinking and Problem-Solving

Critical thinking and problem-solving are among the most vital skills to have in the workplace. They "enable [you] to identify and solve complex problems" (S., 2023). Critical thinking means that you question something, analyze it, interpret your findings, and make a qualified judgment based on everything you gather. By reading this definition, the role of problem-solving becomes clear. You need a lot of critical thinking when trying to find the appropriate solution to any issue. Critical thinking and problem-solving are prerequisites to any career you choose.

Imagine a washing machine company: The top executives need critical thinking skills to plan the expansion of the company while solving problems associated with lack of funding or economic decline. The most junior employee needs critical thinking to perform tasks and solve problems related to customer service. Every element of the workforce is, therefore, based on these skills! When you work on your problem-solving skills, your capacity for critical thinking will increase. As one motivational speaker, Tony Robbins, said, "Every problem is a gift. Without it we wouldn't grow" (Marlin, 2017). As you become older, you'll develop unique ways of solving problems as you gain more experience in your field. However, you can practice the Socratic method as a teen and slowly build this skill. There are four steps in this method:

1. **State the problem.** In this step, you face the challenge head-on and write a clear statement about what the problem is. For example, if you performed badly on a test, write it down. You can write it as you wish, but it's best to keep it short and concise. It may look something like this: "I did not perform well in my history exam."

2. **Find the causes.** In this stage you're tasked with looking for the various reasons explaining the undesirable outcome in Step 1. Ask yourself questions like: *What did I do that led to a poor grade? Am I at fault? Has this happened before?* Write all the reasons down and know that you can overcome them!

3. **Think about solutions.** When you have outlined all the reasons for the unfavorable outcome, be creative and think of how they can be overcome. Ask yourself questions like: *What can I do to avoid it from happening in the future? Is there someone who can help me? How can I change my study practices?* In other words, develop measures you can take to ensure a more effective result in the future.

4. **Implement and review.** During the implementation stage, you put your planned solutions to work. In the example used, you could start studying more, join an afterschool program, or ask your teacher for advice. As you implement them, monitor if your actions are changing your grades. If they are, you're on the right track. If not, you can move back to Step 3 and think of other solutions that will bring you closer to your goal.

This method can be used for any problem that comes your way! If you practice these steps whenever you encounter a problem, it will become second nature and you'll apply it to bigger problems once you're in a career. Nevertheless, critical thinking and problem-solving can be practiced in other ways too. When you actively engage in school activities and the classroom, you will learn from your teachers and friends. Nothing is more valuable than experience, and when you kindly challenge your teacher or friends when you don't agree with them, you'll learn how to stand on your own two feet.

Similarly, you can participate in school clubs or societies that encourage communication and debate. Internships and shadowing are also great opportunities to develop these skills because you'll see how others problem-solve. Maybe you'll even be involved in developing solutions to bigger problems that don't have anything to do with school! It's only when you're met with real-world challenges that you can develop real-world solutions. For this, you need to be creative.

Being in Flow

Critical thinking and problem-solving become more effective when you're in flow. *Flow*, in this context, is defined as "a state of mind in which a person becomes fully immersed in an activity" (Cherry, 2023a). It means that you become so absorbed by your activity that your creativity levels spike and you're performing to the best of your abilities. By being focused on a certain challenge and its possible solutions, you're more likely to be innovative. Simply put, you'll come up with better solutions and learn something in the process. It keeps you engaged and motivated, leading to better performance.

In school or the workplace, flow presents itself as being completely engaged, with all your focus on the topic at hand. For instance, a coder might be so absorbed by a problem on a new computer system that they forget about everything else and work for hours. Oftentimes, someone in flow will forget about the time and work non-stop for hours! When in flow, critical thinking is developed through creativity. You can do several things to achieve flow and train your mind to reach it more easily when in a career.

- One of the most crucial aspects of getting in flow is setting clear goals. It's only when you know what you have to do that the flow can arrive. Use the Socratic method to develop solutions to your specific problem and enact each one with the goal in mind. You can also use other activities to implement the flow. Two examples are reading or playing chess. When you make time for these, you can increase your capacity for concentration.
- Another component is eliminating all distractions when busy with an important activity. Without anything else that requires your attention, you gift yourself the ability to place all emphasis on the problem or situation at hand. Of course, it can be difficult to put your smartphone in another room! Yet, when you set aside time for a specific creative purpose and leave everything else at the door, you have the capacity to become absorbed by the activity requiring critical thinking.
- You should also make the activity challenging. If a solution or activity is too easy, there is no incentive to place all your attention on it. Here, you can try a new activity or hobby that asks you to learn and become better. When completed appropriately, you will feel a sense of fulfillment and be encouraged regarding your abilities. As you try new things and develop new solutions to problems, you can become a more rounded person with a set of critical thinking skills that will benefit you in your future career.

Communication Skills for the Workplace

Effective communication is sometimes described as the secret to success in the workplace. With the expansion of automation and AI, communication may not seem as important. However, one can argue that communication is more essential than ever before. Whether you work in an office or at home, you'll need to collaborate with your bosses, your colleagues, and perhaps customers. For these, you need strong communication skills.

It may come as a surprise to you that a lot of communication deals with aspects other than the spoken word. In fact, some researchers claim that only seven percent of all communication is the words you speak (Michail, 2020). This implies that your tone, ability to listen, and body language are just as important as what you say, if not more. Many mistakenly believe that communication is a simple process whereby you hear what another person says and respond accordingly. They think that listening is a passive process whereby you only focus on the words spoken by someone else and formulate a response. This is false! An effective communicator is an active listener. You can try active listening with your family, friends, and teachers by practicing a few simple rules.

Active Listening

When in a conversation with someone else, ensure that you're fully present. Note this doesn't mean you're only physically there. Instead, show your presence by going closer to the speaking person, turning your body toward them and ignoring other things around them.

Related to this is keeping eye contact. You don't need to stare into their eyes for the duration of the conversation—that can come across as intimidating! Rather, maintain eye contact and only look away for a second or two when necessary. You should also look for any nonverbal cues they give and respond accordingly. For example, if they look down and look embarrassed, adjust your tone to respond more softly. This will show them your support and demonstrate empathy.

If it's your turn to respond, make sure that they're done speaking by asking open-ended questions. Use sentences like "Would you like to expand further?" and "How do you feel about that?" Doing so will open the floor for a deeper conversation. When they're finished, repeat what they told you to show them you understand. Use sentences like, "I hear you're worried," and "I get the sense that you're feeling anxious about this." Don't be judgmental or offer advice if they don't ask you for it. Remember that you're listening to understand, and not only to respond.

Body Language

Alongside listening, you should always focus on your body language. Your body language can either be negative or positive. Negative body language immediately closes you off to the other person and makes you seem unfriendly or disinterested. This could include actions like folding your arms, not maintaining eye contact, or having a tense facial expression. These are certainly problematic in a job interview, but they can cause problems with friends and colleagues as well.

To show positive body language, your posture should be open. This implies that you stand or sit upright—avoiding slouching—with your hands at your sides. When meeting others, give them a firm handshake and look them in the eyes. As soon as you look away, you don't seem as confident as you are! Give subtle smiles and try not to touch your face as this can come across as uncertainty.

Moreover, it's recommended to show interest by nodding your head slowly when someone else speaks and keeping your head upright. You can perhaps even try mirroring. By sometimes copying the actions of the person you're speaking to, you can build a sense of connection. Yet, don't copy all their actions as this can create an uncomfortable atmosphere!

Digital Communication Etiquette

In the past, employees only had to focus on in-person communication with the occasional phone call. Today, most employees have to master online communication as well! There are some tips that can help you handle it well.

Whenever you're in a one-on-one online conversation, always start with the appropriate greeting like "Good morning." This starts the conversation off respectfully and sets the tone of mutual understanding. When the problem or query is solved, be respectful of the other person's time and say goodbye.

In emails and chats, you only have words at your disposal, meaning you can't expect the receiver to know the tone of your message. Therefore, jokes and mixed messages should be avoided at all costs! Be clear and to the point. Read your message a few times to check whether the receiver could be confused as to your actual meaning. This is why emojis and memes should be minimized. Online shorthands like "LOL" and "TTYL" can be confusing to some, especially if the receiver is older. So, spell everything out! Always remember that whatever you write stays on the record and when you make a mistake, your superiors can retrieve it. Hence, proofread all your communications before they're sent, and try not to use the "reply all" feature. You might find it easier, but never forget that you're not talking to the computer. There are human beings on the other side who expect to be treated individually. With these tips, you can be a highly professional online communicator!

Teamwork and Collaboration

A common interview question for all types of jobs centers around a candidate's ability to work in a team. An employer wants to know whether you're able to collaborate with others to meet a company or work goal. The prevalence of this interview question points to the importance of teamwork in the workplace. You probably have experience working with others as school projects sometimes require teamwork. However, you may need some help in becoming a better team player. By answering the following questions honestly, you'll be able to see if this skill needs work:

1. Do you always understand your role when working in a team?
2. Do you welcome advice and feedback from your teammates?
3. Do you hold yourself accountable for all the work you do?
4. Are you flexible in the team? Meaning, can you change your responsibilities when needed?
5. Are you always committed to helping your teammates during the course of the project?

If you answered "No" to any of these, you may need to work on your teamwork skills. Luckily, there are several measures you can take to become better.

Tips to Become a Better Team Player

One of the essentials of being a team player is communication. As you've learned about this earlier, you know what to do! In a team context, your communications should deal with keeping note of your contributions and sharing them with the team. Whenever you have a question, ask your teammates if they have any input on how you can improve. By keeping track of your and your teammates' contributions, everyone will remain focused on the goal you share.

Good communication in a team includes active listening. If you're not the designated leader of the team, you can't be the only one talking!

Give others the opportunity to speak and incorporate what they say into your responses and solutions. Moreover, if conflict erupts, your prior efforts at effective communication will be remembered and the people showing hostility will be more likely to listen to your advice.

You should also offer help when needed. Anyone can become overwhelmed by their tasks and if you lend a helping hand to your teammates, they'll appreciate you. On the flip side, ask for help if you need it.

That said, mutual help is best done in a respectful environment, another tip for optimal teamwork. Understand that every teammate is different and someone may not be as effective as you in a certain task. Practice empathy by encouraging them and asking if you need to clarify something. Think of ways you can support them and listen to their concerns if you see them struggling. Together, you can always come up with a solution.

Some solutions will be hard to come by given the nature of the problem. However, when you confront a challenge early, you'll be more able to avoid repercussions. Schedule frequent meetings with your team and ask them if they suspect any problems you'll encounter in the future. For example, if you're working on a group project in school and someone voices their concern that you won't finish in time, you can work on a new schedule to ensure the deadline is met. Nonetheless, you can still make time for fun! Celebrate your and your teammates' successes by congratulating the team when meeting a certain goal. This optimistic atmosphere is bound to make any team you're in a success!

Leadership Skills for Future Leaders

Leadership skills can be used in any career. The ability to lead others is paramount to success, whether you're a top executive or an intern. As you cultivate qualities that inspire and motivate others, you'll become a great leader. Before learning how you can practice this, you should first know about the different types of leaders there are.

One of the most effective leaders is known as *transformational.* Transformational leaders are good at inspiring others during periods of change and try to help their followers achieve more than they thought possible. On the other hand, *delegative leaders* prefer a hands-off tactic. They like to have a competent team who can use their own creativity, experience and resources to meet certain goals. These leaders don't like to micromanage their team!

Authoritative leadership is the opposite of a delegative leader, as they want to be in full control. This doesn't imply that they're control freaks. Rather, authoritative leaders view themselves as mentors who create a detailed path that the team is expected to follow. They are known to make an effort in personally getting to know all members of the team. *Transactional leaders* operate on a system of rewards and punishments. They like structure and think that team members don't necessarily have the same motivation as they do. This type is also known as "give and take," because the team is motivated by the benefits of completing certain tasks.

Contrarily, *participative leaders* are very interested in their team members and take all their contributions and thoughts into account during the process. They practice active listening and involve everyone in the decision-making process. Lastly, *servant leadership* goes above and beyond in making their team members feel comfortable. They are known to put the needs of others before theirs! Their goal is to make all the team members feel empowered to share their ideas and solutions.

So, how do you know what your leadership style is? You'll only know what you prefer when you put yourself in positions where you're required to lead. Through experience, you'll know what you like and when you listen to the feedback of your team, the answer should become clear. There are cases where you'll be required to choose a certain leadership style because your team members will differ depending on your objectives. Yet, you'll always be drawn to a certain style once you've gone through several collaboration efforts.

Building and Leading Effective Teams

In order to practice your leadership skills, you'll need to grab any opportunity in school or elsewhere that encourages teamwork. Once you're leading a group, you should remember five essential values and build on them.

1. **Get clear on the objective.** Leadership is easiest when everyone involved is united in a common objective. For example, if you're leading a team for a school project, gather everyone together and explain what you'd like to see completed when the team dissolves.
2. **Be direct and transparent.** Schedule daily check-ins to avoid unnecessary confusion or anxiety. You can use instant messaging to your benefit by creating an online group where everyone gives an update once a day. When you're worried about something, let your team members know and ask them for advice.
3. **Increase collaboration.** Sure, your team is working together, but they need to feel like they're part of the team. This means that you encourage them to speak about whatever they want to when not discussing the work at hand. You do this by being

courteous and showing interest in their lives while motivating others to do so as well.

4. **Delegate carefully.** Before giving certain tasks to certain team members, make sure you know what their talents, abilities, and strengths are. When you talk to each member before starting the project, you'll come to know what they'll be best at. This also lessens the possible presence of conflict or jealousy.

5. **Recognize their achievements and be constructive.** When a team member does something well, let them know they're doing a good job. However, when there is conflict or disagreement, schedule a meeting and let everyone talk about their concerns. Try your best to actively listen to their complaints and work on solutions together. If you recognize that a solution won't work out, congratulate the team on their ideas, but explain why you're taking a different approach. If everyone is on the same page, your collaboration can be prosperous. A crucial part of teamwork is emotional intelligence.

Developing Emotional Intelligence

Great leaders have great emotional intelligence. Emotional intelligence gives you the ability to "understand, use, and manage your own emotions in positive ways to relieve stress, communicate effectively, empathize with others, overcome challenges and defuse conflict" (Segal et al., 2024). When this is high, you can effectively use your positive attributes to inspire and motivate others. There are several things you can do to work on your emotional intelligence.

- **First, practice self-awareness through reflection.** Whenever you feel an emotion, label it and try to understand why you're feeling a certain way. Look at your actions and ask yourself:

Why do I do the things I do? Think intensely about your values and explain why you act in a certain manner depending on the situation.

- **Second, practice self-management through personal work.** Not only should you care for your health by eating healthily and exercising, but you should also care for your mental and emotional health. When your thoughts are running away from you, close your eyes and take three deep breaths. This will make you more present and allow you to think about the positives in any scenario.
- **Third, be more socially aware.** Whenever you're interacting with others, remove any distractions and focus solely on the other person. Ask yourself: *What emotions are they displaying? Are they happy or sad?* Be empathetic and compassionate by using positive body language and the active listening tips you learned about. Remember that everyone has a unique life experience and attempt to see things from their point of view. You can even have a "back-pocket" question planned whenever a conversation becomes awkward. Something as simple as "What did you do yesterday?" can be pulled out when you don't know what to say.
- **Last, manage your personal and professional relationships well.** This might sound difficult, but when you practice gratitude for others, they'll see you favorably. Say "Thank you" and verbalize your appreciation to everyone in your life. When you show others you care for them, you admire them, and you're grateful they're in your life, you will be viewed as a positive person. When you build on these four skills, your emotional intelligence will undoubtedly increase, and you'll be an effective leader!

When you work on these skills, you'll be in the best position to find and work in a career that will bring you fulfillment. Remember that you never stop learning and experience is the best tool to uncover these skills. In the next chapter, you're going to learn how you can gain real-world experience!

Key Takeaways

- There are several skills necessary to thrive in your career. Two important ones are critical thinking and problem-solving. A great problem-solving technique is called the Socratic method and consists of four steps: State the problem, find the causes, think about solutions, and implement and review.
- "Being in flow" describes a state of mind during problem-solving that enables you to be completely immersed in an activity. You can achieve the flow by setting clear goals, eliminating any possible distractions, and ensuring the activity is challenging.
- Communication skills are imperative in the workplace. A large part of this is active listening whereby you show the other person you are actively hearing them. You should also have open language by looking the speaker in their eyes and giving positive nonverbal cues. In the digital world, your communications should always be respectful and concise.
- Collaborative skills are also great to have. You can do many things to become a better team player, such as giving your teammates the ability to speak, listening to what they say, offering and asking for feedback, and scheduling regular check-ins.

- You will similarly benefit from having leadership skills. There are various types of leaders—like transformational—and you'll learn what type you are once you're in a leadership position. Some tips to become a better leader include being direct and transparent, delegating carefully, and recognizing the achievements of your teammates.
- As you work with other people, you'll need to have a high level of emotional intelligence. You can develop this by being more self-aware through reflecting on your own emotions and feelings, managing your emotions through relaxing exercises, being more socially aware—like noticing what those around you are feeling—and maintaining your relationships by showing gratitude, to name only one.

CHAPTER 5:

Gaining Real-World Experience

The only source of knowledge is experience. –Albert Einstein

SCHOOL AND COLLEGE TEACH YOU MANY SKILLS necessary for your career. You surely need to know how to read and solve math problems! Yet, one can argue that the valuable lessons you gain from real-world experience are just as crucial as your school and college work. Of course, you need to learn the basics while in the education system, but it's only through doing a certain job that you learn about the actual functioning of the workplace.

Have you ever looked at job postings on websites like LinkedIn? If you have, you'll remember seeing that many employers highlight the requirement of having experience—whether that be a year or more. Even if they don't label it in the job posting, any work experience makes a prospective employee stand out from the crowd. Too often teenagers think that they'll only get experience once they enter the workforce permanently. This thinking is flawed. There are many work opportunities available for teens that you can grasp with both hands and use to make your dream career a reality. Let's learn of a few ways you can gather valuable real-world experience!

Internships: Gateway to Industry Experience

The concept of an internship has been mentioned, but let's give a clear definition. In simple terms, an *internship* is "short-term work experience offered by companies and other organizations for people to get some entry-level exposure to a particular industry or field" (Zhang, 2020). It's a great way to become involved in a career you're interested in without accepting a long-term role with a company.

As you're still in school, an internship allows you to apply what you have learned and builds on your established knowledge. Being an intern comes with a range of benefits. You will learn more about yourself and figure out whether your desired career is the right one for you. You will learn about various types of jobs in a company and perhaps make friends with colleagues who will remember you when you apply for a full-time position. It's essential that you maximize your internship experience should you embark on one. There are some things you need to remember:

- **Start your internship with a few goals.** Ask yourself: *What do I want to learn here? What activities am I already interested in and what can I do to advance these during the internship?* When these goals are set, keep track of your metrics. When you do something well, record your achievement on a document, and when you make a mistake, write down what you learned from it. You could also ask colleagues and your supervisor for feedback regarding how you can perform better.

- **Think about strategic networking.** As soon as you start your internship, identify a few people who are most influential in the company. Look at them closely and see how they lead. Ask yourself questions like: *What leadership style are they following? What skills do they have? And are they respected by their employees?* When you're aware of this, you can create a plan of who you're going to talk to and when. If you show interest in your work with a boss, they're likely to appreciate you and form a connection. This will increase your chances of landing a permanent role in the future.

- **Take time to learn about the workplace culture.** This refers to the "shared values, attitudes, behaviors, and standards that make up a work environment" (Debara, 2022). Look at how your colleagues act and what the bosses generally praise. For example, if you see that a supervisor is always impressed when an employee completes a task quickly, think of ways you can work faster and meet your work goals in a timely manner. Try to build friendships with others by offering to have lunch with another member of your team every day. You will come across as friendly and will bring your unique personality to the office culture.

- **Be proactive.** This means that you seek out opportunities to show off your impressive skills like leadership. Starting a small team-building project or inviting other employees to a small get-together in the office are great ways to leave your mark on the company. You shouldn't wait for your boss or colleague to approach you. Rather, initiate meetings and follow up if your questions aren't answered. You'll come across as strong and determined!

When you follow these tips, you'll have a better chance of transitioning from an intern to an employee. The key to success in this regard is adapting to the earlier mentioned workplace culture. If you identify what the company respects and act in accordance with it, you'll seem like a good addition to the team. Try to continue learning and growing in the company by asking for feedback and offering it to your supervisors. When interacting with your team, demonstrate your values by always ensuring that you put out quality work and exceed their expectations.

No one will ever criticize you for doing more than they asked. Moreover, don't be afraid of showing interest. By being clear on your goal of potentially joining the company full-time, you'll show yourself to be decisive and serious. You don't need to be worried about asking your boss for a full-time job in the future. Chances are likely that they'll see your determined nature and want you to join! Maybe the most important aspect is to build and maintain your workplace relationships. If you seem like a kind, loyal, and caring person, people will remember you and your boss will be open to offering you a permanent position. Just be yourself and exercise your wonderful qualities daily!

Finding an Internship

You might be surprised at how easy it is to find an internship. There are a variety of options available to you. When you try one and have trouble finding an opportunity, go another route without becoming discouraged. There are four avenues you can take.

1. **Find connections through family and friends.** Many internships operate by word-of-mouth, meaning you can talk to others and see if they know of any opportunities. A great tip is to think of people you know who are currently in a career you

aspire to. Get in contact with them and find out if they can speak to their company about a potential role for teens.

2. **Speak to your school counselor or teacher.** Oftentimes, schools have professional relationships with businesses in your area. When you ask your school counselor for advice, they might be able to get you into contact with a company you're interested in. This requires you to be proactive by setting up a meeting.
3. **Research businesses in your area and contact them.** You may be a bit shy when speaking to people you don't know, but the rewards will definitely be worth it. Send an email or phone a company close to you and ask if they have internship opportunities for teens. You could even go there personally and talk to the secretary who can put you in contact with the employer.
4. **Use the internet.** This has been briefly mentioned but begs repeating. If you have access to the internet, you can scour through hundreds of internship opportunities. Four great websites are Indeed, Chegg Internships, Monster, and Glassdoor. All of them regularly upload internship openings.

Volunteering

When people think about volunteering, they don't usually think about gaining work experience. The term *volunteering* is almost naturally thought of as "charity." Although this is partly correct, volunteering is a great source of real-world experience. There are many benefits of volunteering for your future career. A prominent one is that it helps you think about your work goals. As one expert wrote, "Volunteering presents a non-threatening opportunity for you to figure out [what you want to do]" (Boogard, 2020). For example, if you are drawn to a future career in geology or wildlife, volunteering at a local zoo or animal facility can either validate or dismiss this plan.

Similarly, volunteering helps you refine your skills. Volunteering in something that interests you encourages you to learn more about a topic before you need to make a decision regarding college or post-school education. Not only that, but volunteering expands your social network as you build connections with people in your desired field. This leads to greater personal confidence in your abilities and increases your self-worth. Giving back to the community while you build your skills is a win-win scenario! Being a volunteer motivates you to collaborate with like-minded individuals and expands your professional network.

Perhaps the most poignant advantage of volunteering is that it looks impressive on your resume. In fact, one study found that 82% of employers said that they "prefer applicants with volunteer experience" (Fisher, 2016). Being a volunteer looks impressive to prospective employers for several reasons. First, it shows that you take initiative and that you're a hard worker. By taking time out of your day to do something helpful—that you have no financial incentive to do—a company can see that you have personal and professional drive. Second, it proves that you're empathetic with a high regard for service and communication. As volunteering is generally a team effort, a boss will know that you have the capacity to work with others, with a possible ability to lead effectively. And third, volunteering provides you with references. Employers always want to come in contact with people a candidate has worked with before. If you have worked in other organizations, an employer can contact your previous colleagues and hear about your attributes and skills.

There is no set rule on where to place your volunteering endeavors on your resume. Yet, it's most powerful when you put them under a heading labeled "Experience" or create a subheading titled "Volunteering." You can't go wrong by giving back to society!

Identifying Skill-Building Volunteer Opportunities

You have many volunteering options to choose from. However, it's best to look for opportunities that relate to the skills you're trying to build. For example, if you envision a career in public service, your interpersonal skills can be developed by volunteering for the Red Cross. The first step in your volunteering journey is, therefore, knowing what your career goals are. Think about the skills needed to succeed in your desired job and create a list of the types of volunteering opportunities where they can be strengthened.

After identifying these skills, do some research by asking your teachers and friends for advice on where you can offer a helping hand. Your personal investigation can also include some online research. By reading up on a few organizations on the internet, you'll find various openings.

The only thing left to do after that is to contact them and ask if they'll be open to meeting with you. There are countless nonprofit organizations that are always looking for volunteers, including Habitat for Humanity, Key Club, Meals on Wheels, the Red Cross, and Best Buddies. You'll find their websites in the online resources at the end of the chapter!

Part-Time Jobs: Learning on the Job

Another great activity for gaining real-world experience is getting a part-time job. This differs from volunteering because, in most cases, you get paid for your services. Of course, getting a part-time job is more difficult than volunteering because a company or business will look for necessary skills and interview other prospective employees. A part-time job is also more intensive, meaning that you'll have strict hours and a list of tasks you're expected to complete effectively. Making a lot of mistakes is therefore discouraged and you'll be managed in the same way as a full-time employee.

Many teens avoid part-time jobs because it requires more dedication and planning than volunteering. Yet, by following a few basic guidelines, a part-time job can benefit you in many ways. There are three things you should remember to strike a healthy balance between work and school.

1. **Get organized.** Working part-time while you're still at school requires a lot of planning. Your class and work schedules need to be organized so that there is no overlap, and each gets the attention it deserves. It's best to create a to-do list before the week starts and allocate time for all your responsibilities. Use an Excel spreadsheet to create an outline of your upcoming week and stick to the rules you set out.
2. **Take breaks and remove distractions.** Your Excel spreadsheet should make time for things you enjoy. If you're always at school or at work, you have no time to relax. Relaxing is very important for your health and combats fatigue and a lack of motivation. On the flip side, while you're busy at work or at school, place your phone and anything else that threatens your concentration away from reach. Work on one thing at a time and try not to think about what task you have to do next.
3. **Always communicate and ask for help.** You have many people in your life who care about you. If you feel overwhelmed at school or at work, talk to your teacher or colleague. They might offer advice on how you can organize better. Don't be afraid to ask for help if you need it and remember that you're still

learning. You don't have to be perfect when starting a part-time job. The longer you balance your work and school responsibilities, the better you'll become at giving your best to both!

Like volunteering, your part-time job should optimally use the skills you'll need in a future career. That way, you can transfer these skills to the full-time job you want when you're finished with school or college. For example, by taking a part-time job in customer service, you'll work on your communication skills, which will benefit you in a career in social services. Before applying to part-time jobs, think deeply about how the skills you'll use there will benefit your desired career. Nonetheless, you'll surely learn many basic skills—like time management—in any part-time job. Thus, don't be *overly* specific when applying for a job while in high school. Any effort in joining the workforce while you're still a teen will be favorable to your career.

How to Find a Part-Time Job

Finding a part-time job is similar to finding an internship, in that you'll need to go for an interview and put your best foot forward. However, part-time jobs are frequently advertised in more traditional ways. This means that you can look for openings in the newspaper and local community job boards in the library. Sometimes, businesses in your city or town will have signs indicating that they're looking for help. For instance, a local restaurant might hang a sign that reads "Hiring servers." You can also tell your family and friends that you're hoping to find a part-time job and they can help by keeping their eyes out for signs or postings like these.

That said, you can use the many available technical tools as well! By searching for online community hubs and researching companies you're interested in, you can come in contact with possible recruiters.

Websites like LinkedIn are also available with several postings being for hourly or short-term work. A great website for American teens is Snagajob. This online marketplace focuses on hourly work and posts many part-time jobs for teens. You can create an account and start your search today! Always remember that rejection doesn't mean there's something wrong with you. There are many businesses that would love to have you on their team!

Summer Jobs

Summer jobs are given a bad rap. People don't give them the credit they deserve! Summer jobs usually don't require a lot of skill and include activities such as mowing lawns or running errands for someone. This might not seem like work-related experience, but the opposite is true. A summer job not only brings in some money, but it encourages you to develop soft skills that can be applied to any career. Soft skills are defined as "general characteristics, relevant to personality traits" (Pavlou, 2019). For example, time management and endurance in a work environment. Therefore, the type of summer job you take might not be as important as the skills you develop while doing it.

A significant advantage of a summer job is that it boosts your confidence. As you're taken out of your comfort zone, you'll become more self-reliant and realize that you can do anything you set your mind to. It also helps you recognize what you enjoy and what kind of activities you thrive in. You also broaden your circle by interacting with different people and building a clientele that might put in a good word for you when looking for permanent employment. You can make the most of your summer job by using the following tips:

- **Start any summer job with a set of clear goals.** Before starting a summer job, think about what you want to achieve and what skills you want to foster. If you identify that you need to work on your communication skills, make plans on how you'll interact with a customer. Write down some phrases you're going to say and think of how you'll come across to them. Additionally, think of how your summer job will look on your resume and what skills you'll have upon its completion.

- **Try to remain positive.** Treat every day of your summer job as a learning opportunity! When you're heading to work, think of a few things you want to achieve that day. Ask yourself: *What will I be proud of this evening? And what can I do to ensure this day is well spent?* Keep your eyes focused on the future if you need to do something you don't enjoy. Bad experiences are part of the journey!

- **Be professional and excel in your role.** Sure, you're not going to like all the tasks you need to do; however, always remain courteous and professional. If you encounter a serious problem, address it with the customer and frame it in such a way that you want to develop a mutual solution. This will create a positive work environment while making you seem interested in the job they gave you.

- **Build connections and celebrate all your achievements.** The more summer jobs you do, the larger the pool of people you can choose from when seeking permanent employment. Although someone might not have a full-time role, a customer may put you in contact with potential employers. You don't need to forge friendships with customers, but you should always put your best foot forward and communicate with them. If you do a good job, they'll recognize you as a reliable and trustworthy person. Be proud of everything you accomplish and do something fun when you meet a certain goal!

Landing a Summer Job

Summer jobs are the least likely to be published online. The vast majority of openings travel by word of mouth. This means that you'll have to be creative in landing a summer job that will provide meaningful experiences and contribute to your career readiness. Once again, the importance of networking arises. When speaking to adults and teachers, they'll give you advice and put you in contact with prospective employers. Nevertheless, you can still make use of online search platforms. You'll be much more effective if you start looking early. Find out when the last day of school is on your academic calendar—normally it's in June in the United States—and ensure that you start searching two months before that.

Many teens will be looking for a job when school ends, but if you're first, your chances of landing a summer job will increase. In addition, do some research on seasonal businesses. A lot of companies see a surge of clients during summer and desperately need extra help. By looking for opportunities at local museums, restaurants, or zoos, you'll have a greater chance of finding something. Family-oriented businesses are promising options as well. Also called mom-and-pop stores, these businesses value contributions from their communities and usually want to help local teens who need experience. Places like hardware stores, bakeries, and supermarkets are wonderful places to enter the workforce! If you make use of all these tools, you're bound to find a summer job that builds your skillset.

Even though networking has been mentioned quite a few times in this chapter, a deeper look into this promising career component will help you immeasurably. In the next chapter, you're going to learn about the importance of networking and mentorship!

Key Takeaways

- What you learn from real-world experiences is as important—if not more—as your schoolwork. There are many opportunities available to you, with one being an internship. An internship is defined as "short-term work experience offered by companies and other organizations for people to get some entry-level exposure to a particular industry or field" (Zhang, 2020).
- Internships require you to be proactive, and once you find an opportunity, your capacity for networking and learning about workplace cultures will increase. You can find an internship by asking family, friends, and teachers. You can also use the internet by making use of websites like Chegg Internships and Glassdoor.
- Volunteering is a great way to gain experience while helping your community. It is also great to have on your resume because it proves you take the initiative and are a determined person. You can search for volunteering opportunities in the same manner you would internships. There are many websites you can use, such as Habitat for Humanity and the Red Cross.
- Part-time jobs are usually the most intensive for teens because you're expected to do your schoolwork while working in your free time. If you start a part-time job, you should be organized, take breaks when needed, and always communicate and ask for help if needed. You can find a part-time job by looking online and asking around in your community.
- Summer jobs are great tools for gaining work experience. This might be the easiest option for you because you'll only need to work during your school vacation. Tips to succeed in a summer job include setting goals, remaining positive, being professional,

and building connections with your customers. Summer jobs can be found in various ways, like online postings and keeping an eye on "Help Wanted" signs in local businesses.

Online Resources

- **American Red Cross:** https://www.redcross.org/
- **Best Buddies:** https://www.bestbuddies.org/
- **Chegg Internships:** https://www.chegg.com/
- **Glassdoor:** https://www.glassdoor.com/index.htm
- **Habitat for Humanity:** https://www.habitat.org/
- **Indeed:** https://www.indeed.com/
- **Key Club:** https://www.keyclub.org/
- **LinkedIn:** https://www.linkedin.com/
- **Meals on Wheels:** https://www.mealsonwheelsamerica.org/
- **Monster:** https://www.monster.com/
- **Snagajob:** https://www.snagajob.com/

CHAPTER 6:

Networking and Mentorship

The number one unwritten rule of success is networking. –Sallie Krawcheck

DID YOU KNOW THAT AN ESTIMATED 70% OF JOB openings in the United States are never published publicly (Zane, 2022)? This means that the majority of employment positions are never posted on LinkedIn or in the newspaper! This might sound confusing, but there are two reasons for this. First, many companies prefer to hire someone already employed by them to fill a new position. For example, an intern—if they did their job well—will be interviewed for a full-time position when the internship ends. And second, numerous job fillings rest solely on networking.

Whether you're looking for a job or progressing in your career, professional networking is crucial. In fact, a survey found that 79% of American employees believe networking contributed overwhelmingly to their present careers (Zane, 2022). The importance of networking is also related to mentorship whereby you get guidance from experienced professionals. There are myriad stories about people who started small and were mentored by their colleagues, allowing them to land a bigger role in the company. Mark Thompson, the CEO of the Cable News Network (CNN), began his career as a young production trainee with the British Broadcasting Corporation (BBC)! Networking and mentorship are certainly cornerstones of professional success. Let's look at the basics of professional networking first!

The Basics of Professional Networking

Professional networking is something that scares many teens because it asks you to put yourself out there and build connections with strangers. It might be daunting to begin the process of networking, but as you develop these skills, it'll come naturally over time. Interacting with others to advance your career is also called *strategic networking*, defined as, "a deliberate and focused approach to building a network of contacts and relationships that can help individuals or organizations achieve their goals" (Persona, 2023). In other words, you progress in your career by forming connections with people who can help you make your goals a reality.

Setting up a networking plan is critical because it serves as a personal roadmap that guides you toward your desired career. If you neglect this aspect in the professional world, you're less likely to succeed. Even if you start a business—something that calls on you to depend solely on yourself—you'll still need to connect with investors, customers, and other businesses in your area. There are six steps in building your professional networking strategy.

1. **Set your networking goals.** By using the earlier mentioned SMART system, set a few goals of what you want to achieve by networking. These goals will serve as the compass for all your

networking actions. Ask yourself questions like: *Who will advance my career? Who can be a mentor and teach me the necessary skills to thrive in my desired job? And who might be a potential employer or customer in the future?* When these goals are set, you'll be more effective in performing the second step.

2. **Look for your ideal connections.** With your goals in mind, look for people who align with them. By doing some research and finding industry leaders or influential employees of a company you're interested in, you'll gather a few names. Write all these names down and assess how they'll be able to help you in realizing your career goals. Stay up to date on what's happening in your career field by searching for the latest news on the company and by reading the LinkedIn profiles of your potential connections.

3. **Plan your outreach tactics.** In this step, you should start thinking of how you'll reach out to the people you identified. Namely, how are you going to initiate contact? You can choose traditional ways, like a call, or modern ways, such as leveraging social media. When planning this, ensure that you modify all your communications independently. This means that you do enough research on the person, identify what they value, and come up with ideas of what they will want to see in you. For example, if you read that a certain industry leader is environmentally conscious, think of ways how you can include this interest in the email or message you send them. This will form an instant connection over shared interests.

4. **Create your first interaction.** First impressions are everything! Several studies have indicated that it takes only three seconds for someone to decide whether to do business with you (Giang, 2014). Although this finding was based on in-person meetings,

your email, call, or message should be perfect as well. When you've found a way of reaching your hopeful connection, show genuine interest in what they do, be respectful, and suggest ways that your collaboration will benefit both of you. This doesn't mean you should immediately make demands. Rather, you can form initial contact by commenting on something positive they've done.

5. **Cultivate the connection.** After your initial contact, foster the connection and keep communication alive. If they responded kindly to your email, call, or message, continue with the conversation. Here, it's essential that you find balance. You don't want to swarm their inbox with endless messages, but you want to ensure that they remember you. When you message them, it can be helpful to ask something specific and achievable. People are far more likely to respond to a clear request that they can easily accommodate rather than a more general request. Perhaps there's an event coming up that they're hosting that you could request a pass for, or you could ask them to shadow a member of their team for half a day. Remember, "networking is a marathon, not a sprint" (Persona, 2023). It might take some time until your communications become more regular, but the more the person reciprocates, the faster you can continue the conversation.
6. **Evaluate your communications.** Networking never ceases, and you should constantly re-evaluate whether your interactions with the person are helping you progress toward your career goals. Moreover, don't become so absorbed by communication with one person that you neglect others. The bigger the number of people you speak to, the better your chances of meeting your career objectives. Stay on the lookout for more contacts while making sure that the quality of your relationships with current

contacts remains intact. By evaluating your networking success, you'll see what's working, what can be done better, and how effective your manners of communication are.

Creating an Elevator Pitch

As you've read, follow-ups are vital to nurturing relationships. Yet, their responses are more likely to occur if you introduce yourself with an effective elevator pitch during your initial contact. An *elevator pitch* refers to "a quick synopsis of your background, experiences, and purpose" (Doyle, 2024). It essentially tells your prospective contact more about yourself so that they have a good idea of who you are and, hopefully, how you will benefit their own career goals.

Elevator pitches usually refer to a speech you give when you go for an interview. However, they can also be modified to apply to an email or any other online tool. There are a few rules you should follow in developing your unique elevator pitch.

- Your elevator pitch should always start with what you do. A good tip before writing this is to think about what you want the person to remember about you. Someone may not remember what you say, but they'll always remember your enthusiasm for what you do! After you've written this, ask yourself: *Does this excite me?* If it does, the receiver is more likely to notice your passion and respond.
- After you've done this, develop your USP—unique selling proposition. Namely, what makes you special? While writing this, compare yourself to others and explain why you're unique. This doesn't mean you're being boastful. Rather, it shows that you believe in yourself, and the other person will benefit from having a connection with you.

- Follow your USP with an intriguing, open-ended question. This is intended to engage your reader or listener and involve them in the conversation. Your question should not have a "yes" or "no" answer, but it should make them think. For example, if you're contacting an industry leader, ask them "What do you envision for the future of your company?" Make sure that you've thought about your recommendations if they reply!
- When all of these components are developed, put them together and review your elevator pitch. What can be changed? What sentences can be more effective? Do you think the receiver will be impressed? Spend some time reading through everything and edit the areas where you think necessary. You can ask your family or teachers to take a look at your pitch and listen to their advice. Remember that your pitch shouldn't be too wordy. The receiver will be more impressed with a short, effective message than a long document or speech!

Mentorship

Networking and mentorship are quite different concepts. Whereas networking refers to building and maintaining communication with people who can help advance your career, mentorship refers to learning from someone. *Mentorship* is broadly defined as "an intentional effort to support, encourage, and/or motivate someone in a particular space who has less experience [and] creativity than you do in that space" (Fall, 2022). Using this definition, the person teaching you is a mentor, and you are the mentee. In your career, a mentor will teach you the necessary skills and talents you need to succeed. You can benefit from a mentor-mentee relationship in any job you do as a teen, such as an internship or a summer job. In establishing your relationship with a mentor, you have to follow a few rules.

- **Lay the groundwork.** Unlike networking, finding a mentor is usually done in person. You can only learn effectively when you're actively working with your mentor in the real world! When you identify who you want your mentor to be, schedule a meeting with them, while remaining respectful of their time and other obligations. You may need to follow up if they don't respond to your first request. The location of the meeting should be somewhere where you won't be bothered.
- **Tell them what you want to learn.** When you're meeting with your prospective mentor, tell them what you admire about them and indicate what you want to learn. Explain why you chose them by pointing to their accomplishments and admirable characteristics. When they talk to you, practice active listening and incorporate what they tell you in your responses. Moreover, develop solutions when they have reservations, such as the amount of time they'll be able to spend with you.
- **Build a connection.** As you tell them what you want to learn, give them an overview of your experiences, dreams, and areas of hopeful expertise. Tell them about your ideas for your future and how—you believe—they can be instrumental in helping you meet your goals. They will probably tell you about their own experiences and who mentored them. Ask them questions about this and have a notepad handy to write down anything that comes to mind. This will prove your dedication to the hopeful relationship and build trust on which the mentor-mentee relationship can be based.
- **Develop shared expectations.** If your first meeting was successful and your mentor agreed to teach you, develop some shared goals as a team. As you're the one who sought the relationship, the responsibility falls on you to come up with a

game plan first. For example, you can discuss meeting once every two weeks or once a month. Ensure that you run this by your mentor and ask if they think this is adequate. Ask them what they want to see from you and what you can do to advance their lessons in your personal time. You can also ask them what they think are the most important things you need to learn. Doing so will start the relationship with several goals and the mentor will also begin to brainstorm on what teaching methods will be most effective.

- **Plan your communication channels in person.** With these goals in mind, you and your mentor have to prepare the ways in which you'll communicate with each other. Here, questions like where they are based, your school schedule, and personal responsibilities arise. Is it possible to have regular phone calls, and what times are both of you available? Do you have the technology to have video calls? Or, if you work in the same office, can you use lunch breaks for learning sessions? If you develop collaborative communication rules, you should stick to them. Being clear on your mode of communication will foster continued support and learning!

Finding a Mentor

Finding your personal mentor will be a unique experience. Of course, you should first look at what you want to learn. When you know this, you can create a list of possible mentors. For example, if you have a summer job in a restaurant because you want to work in the culinary field, the head chef can be your mentor. It's best to look for mentors in your workplace—or your desired workplace—because this will allow for in-person meetings.

Use your newly found networking skills to contact potential mentors based on your own research. It's essential that your mentor has the experience you want to gain. For instance, if you want to work in the corporate world and your aunt has been a financial manager for 20 years, she's probably a good candidate! Once you've chosen a mentor and have a meeting set up, think of some questions you can ask them. You can use the five following questions, as they'll give you a glimpse into your mentor's expertise.

1. What professional experience has led to your current position?
2. What skills do you think are most important in this career field?
3. What do you think are three important things I need to learn about this career field?
4. What inspires you in your career field, and do you think I would feel the same way if I joined this field?
5. What are some challenges in this career field?

Using Social Media for Networking

Social media is a great tool to network with industry professionals, or with any business you'd like to work with in the future. Think about social media as the new town square where you can make your presence known and impress professional contacts! Practically all companies and industry leaders have profiles on social media. In fact, many LinkedIn profiles have links to their Facebook, Instagram, or X profiles. Use these for your research and—when you're ready—contact purposes.

When you find someone you want to be in contact with, learn more about them before reaching out. This means that you do some research on who they are, what company they work for, how a relationship with them will advance your hopeful career, and what values they espouse. Only after this is done should you send them a personalized message. Remember that they probably get numerous messages if they're well-known, making your first impression extremely important. Use your unique elevator pitch to draw them in! Moreover, ensure that your message isn't too long as this will run the risk of them getting bored. They're probably busy and will only want to take a quick look.

In addition to contacting individuals, you can engage with industry content. Before doing this, make sure that your goals are clearly outlined and that you find the relevant industries associated with them. For example, if you're interested in engineering, search for the social media pages of local engineering companies. After you've found them, be interactive. When the company or leader posts something, comment on it and tell them why you think it's great. You can also share their articles with a wider audience and tag them when you post something related to their industry.

This brings up the importance of hashtags. You probably know that when you post hashtags with a keyword, the poster can see it. Whenever you achieve a goal or make a contribution to their industry, use the hashtag to bring their attention to your profile. This will increase your visibility and prove your expertise in their field. Hopefully, they see it and will remember you when you reach out personally! If you want to leave a lasting impression, it's crucial that you build a professional online profile.

Building a Professional Online Profile

In the technological age we live in, your online profile serves as one of the most essential aspects of your career. Your online profile is an extension of you and shows professional strangers who you are without meeting in person. For this reason, your profile should be immaculate. The online landscape is similar to the real world, in that people look at you and make an impression upon seeing you. You wouldn't walk in the mall while wearing pajamas! Why would you then not look and act your best online? When looking to enter the job market or prepare for a future career, your online profile is the gateway to success. When setting up an online profile—that will leave the reader impressed—you should remember a few things.

- **Know what platforms you want to join.** There are endless options you have to showcase your skills and talents. Of course, websites like LinkedIn will open you up to job opportunities. However, if you want to network with those in your field, you can create professional profiles on websites like YouTube, Instagram, X, and Facebook. Although these may not seem professional in nature, prospective employers and companies all have profiles and interactions on them. It's best to have two profiles—one personal and one professional. If you create a profile solely based on your career goals, you'll come across as determined.
- **Show your value.** When you've chosen your platforms, create a profile by adding a professional picture. People always want to see what you look like! This picture should not be a selfie, and you shouldn't look too casual. You can either have a professional picture taken, or you can ask a loved one to take one of you wearing semi-formal clothing in front of a plain backdrop. Preface your profile with a short paragraph—no more than 10 sentences—about who you are and what your professional values are. Follow this with a short list of your skills, possible experience, and interests. It's best to correlate your values to those promoted by companies in your field of

choice. This will create a lasting impression on the leaders you hope to work with!

- **Display your personality in all your interactions.** Once your profile is up and running, you should be very active and show what kind of person you are. This means that you post articles about the industry you want to enter, comment on posts by possible networking candidates, and post statuses surrounding your desired field. It's best to avoid anything that pertains to other topics such as politics. Instead, post about your achievements and hobbies as they relate to your career field. You should always seem enthusiastic and refrain from using offensive language that would insult your audience. Visual elements are also very powerful. For example, if you receive an award at school showcasing a skill, post the certificate and tell your audience how this will help you achieve your goals. Try to avoid fake profiles and always talk to your parents if you receive an unusual message or request from someone who seems untrustworthy.
- **Modify, modify, modify.** While you're advancing your profile and interacting with others, you should remain open to modifying your profile. If you learn something new that makes a prior statement on your profile redundant, remove it. If you have a better picture after a month of being online, replace the old one. The more you network, the more you'll find what they're looking for. This can guide you to make necessary changes and perfect your profile to suit the needs of your desired field. An article on LinkedIn states, "Your online profile is not a static document, but a dynamic and evolving reflection of your career path" (*How do You Make Your Online Profile Work for You*, n.d.). Therefore, update your profile

regularly and make the most of the technological age you live in!

Attending Industry Conferences and Workshops

While looking online, you may also find events and conferences in your desired career field. Professional events are great locations for networking and learning more about your future career. Work conferences are often free of charge and are posted online. If you find one and are able to get to it, you should go!

Moreover, when you're at the event, your goal should be to be an active participant. You'll certainly learn a lot, but if your goal is to network as well, you have to prepare for conversations. Before you attend, develop some questions that you want to ask speakers. These can surround topics like skills and what they think you should do to succeed.

Sometimes, speakers will allow for questions during a session. If you're wary of speaking in front of many people, you can wait for the session to finish and go to the speaker afterward. Introduce yourself kindly and tell them what you enjoyed about their speech before asking them your questions. Have a notepad ready and write their answers down. Not only will this help you remember what they said, but it will impress the speaker and make you seem curious.

Don't only focus on the speakers, though. Many professionals and other people—of a similar age to you—attend these events to learn more about their field. Speak to some of them during a lunch break or a socializing event after the speeches. Initiate conversations, talk about yourself, and ask questions to build professional friendships. It's a good idea to take down their contact information or ask about their online profiles to keep collaboration going. When the conference is finished, contact them again and use the event as a springboard from which you can discuss other matters.

If you message a speaker who impressed you, tell them what you liked about their speech and what you learned from them. If you have a part-time job or are busy with an internship, share what you learned from the conference and perhaps ask your boss about their recommendations on where you should go next.

Networking is something you should work on full-time and the more events you partake in, the greater the pool of professionals you can draw from when building your career path. You can't go wrong by making time to learn from the best and by building relationships at career-related events!

Finding Conferences and Events

You might be surprised at how easy it is to find conferences and events for networking and learning purposes. All you need is a plan and to follow a few steps. As you move through these steps and attend various events, you'll become familiar with the process and be more confident in forging relationships with industry leaders and mentors. There are four steps!

1. **Think about what you need to learn and do.** Before thinking of which conferences you want to attend, take a deep look at what your goals are. Do you want to meet some influential people in the field? Do you want to learn more about a certain career? Do you want to know what skills you need to develop? Identify what types of events carry the most rewards. This will narrow your options down and guide you toward the type of conference you should attend.

2. **Investigate the options.** Many industries host frequent conferences and finding one is easy. After identifying what your goals are, ask your family or friends about events they know about. Using online resources can be very effective. You can scour through the social media pages of various companies, look at their official websites, or check if they have newsletters. They will always post about an upcoming event with information regarding its location, who the speakers will be, and how long it will be. Your company or organization of choice will post it on LinkedIn, but if you want a variety of options, you can take advantage of other online platforms like Meetup and Eventbrite. You can use these websites to search for possible conferences!

3. **Organize your materials.** When you've chosen the event or conference you want to take part in, ensure that you have everything you need. This means that you must check whether you should reserve a ticket, plan your transportation, and choose the speeches you'll attend. Additionally, have your documents ready! These include your resume, possible business cards, and contact information that you can give to those you'll network with. You can also prepare some questions and research the backgrounds of the companies or speakers who'll be attending. Lastly, plan your outfit. Look impressive by wearing semiformal attire that shows you mean business!

4. **Attend the event.** With all this planning, the only thing left is to go learn, network, and enjoy yourself. While networking, focus on building long-lasting relationships by being friendly, showing interest, and handing your contact information to others who attend. Use the communication skills you developed in Chapter 4 and impress anyone you speak with by showcasing your research about the event. They have to see genuine passion when you engage in conversations with them. Talk about what you're

enjoying about the conference and how you think this will advance your career. Remember to have fun while you're busy networking! Sure, you'll be a bit nervous if you haven't attended a conference before, but just be yourself and anyone you speak to is bound to find you intriguing!

Networking can certainly play a pivotal role in helping you land the job of your dreams! That being said, what if you want to become an entrepreneur? Starting a side hustle while you're in school requires a unique set of skills and actions. In the next chapter, you'll learn the art of the side hustle!

Key Takeaways

- Networking is imperative in finding a job in your desired career field. *Professional networking* is defined as "a deliberate and focused approach to building a network of contacts and relationships that can help individuals or organizations achieve their goals" (Persona, 2023).
- There are six steps in building a professional networking strategy. They are setting your networking goals, looking for ideal connections, planning your outreach tactics, having your first interaction, cultivating the connection, and evaluating your communications.
- All your networking efforts need to be prefaced with an elevator pitch that gives the other person a summary of who you are. A verbal or written elevator pitch must include the following: An explanation of what you do, your unique selling proposition (USP), and an open-ended question.

- Mentorship is as important as networking and refers to a relationship with an experienced person who teaches you about your job or career. You can establish a relationship with a mentor of your choice by laying the groundwork—identifying a mentor and introducing yourself, telling them what you want to learn, building a connection, developing shared expectations, and planning how you'll communicate with each other.
- You can use social media—and various online profiles—to network with people in your desired career field. You are more likely to attract someone's attention if you have a professional online profile. In developing your online profile, you should know what platforms you want to join, show your values, portray your personality through posts and comments, and modify your profile when necessary.
- Networking can also be done at conferences and career events. To find a conference or event, you can follow a few steps: think about who you want to network with, investigate the event options and choose one, organize all your materials, such as your resume and business cards, and go to the event.

Online Resources

- **Eventbrite:** https://www.eventbrite.com/
- **Facebook:** https://www.facebook.com/
- **LinkedIn:** https://www.linkedin.com/
- **Meetup:** https://www.meetup.com/
- **X:** https://twitter.com/?lang=en

CHAPTER 7:

The Art of the Side Hustle

A side hustle can provide the extra income you need to fund your dreams. – Unknown

SIDE HUSTLES ARE GREAT OPPORTUNITIES FOR TEENS. A *side hustle* is defined as, "a flexible job that you work at 'to the side' of your primary job" (Team Everlance, 2022). As you're still a teen, your primary "job" is probably going to school! Therefore, a side hustle for you refers to something you do in your free time that exercises your entrepreneurial spirit. For example, if you create homemade jewelry and sell them in your community or online.

A side hustle differs from a summer job or a part-time job because it implies that you start something from scratch and don't rely on an employer to pay you for your services. Simply put, you go at it alone. Side hustles can teach you various skills and might even lead to your own fully functional business in the future.

There are many stories of people who grew their side hustles into amazing careers. Martha Stewart, a famous businesswoman in the hospitality industry, started a catering business in her basement while working as a stockbroker in 1976. Her business grew so large that her net worth was an estimated $400 million in 2020! (Cassell, 2022). If you're looking to start a side hustle, you should identify your entrepreneurial interests first. Let's find out how!

Identifying Your Entrepreneurial Interests

Any side hustle you begin is more likely to succeed if you identify what you're really passionate about. Sure, you can start a small side job with the sole purpose of making some money. Yet when you find something that inspires you, you'll be motivated and encouraged to grow the business. Getting an income for doing something you love is a dream come true! When you enjoy an activity and find a way to monetize it, it will feel like a hobby—as opposed to a job—that brings you satisfaction. The success of a side hustle depends on the amount of time you're willing to put into it, and when it truly interests you, you won't even notice the hours you spend on developing your product or service. In exploring your passions with the goal of starting a side hustle there are three things you should remember.

1. **Ask yourself what you're curious about.** Don't think too far into the future. Rather, focus on what you like doing right now and read up on it. Ask yourself: *What is something I like that others don't? And what are my interests that don't seem like the norm for my age group?* When you search your interests that aren't obvious career decisions, you will unlock your creativity!
2. **Money should not be your primary goal.** As mentioned earlier, a side hustle is more likely to be successful if you aren't

overly concerned about the income. You should aim to follow your curiosity without worrying too much about how much you'll make. This might sound paradoxical, but if you start a side hustle you're really interested in, you will do your best to ensure a good product or service. The motivation from truly caring about your side hustle pushes you toward developing it further. Development and creativity lead to a competitive product or service that more people will want.

3. **Don't be afraid to change course.** The great thing about a side hustle is that you can always leave it or make changes. If you identify your passions and work on an entrepreneurial endeavor associated with it, you can always modify it or scrap it completely. You have the ability to make changes, create a new product, or take on something new if you realize it's not working out well. You're still young. Try different things and see what brings you the greatest rewards!

Once you start a side hustle, your product or service will probably change over time. For example, if you want to sell second-hand clothing online, you'll do more research as the business grows and change the ways you conduct your work. You experiment with your business by trying new things and removing activities that don't bring you toward your entrepreneurial goals. You should always be aware of the *feedback loop*, defined as, "the process of collecting, analyzing, and implementing feedback, and then using those learnings to make your future work better" (Skusa, 2022).

Your side hustle will always remain in a state of trial and error, meaning you'll make mistakes. The key is to keep updated on how your product or service is being used and experienced by your customers. When you use their feedback—by taking note of their compliments and complaints—you should use these to make your side hustle even better. By welcoming feedback when your side hustle is still small, you can make the necessary changes as your business grows.

Market Research

You need to conduct research before you embark on any side hustle. *Market research* "is the process of gathering data about people or companies and analyzing it to figure out what they're looking for" (Keenan, 2024).

Although your side hustle should be based on your passions and interests, you have to take the needs and wants of your community into account. Your business is bound to thrive if you find a gap in the market and can give them something that isn't readily available. This also means that you take note of your competition and how your product or service can be better than theirs. People generally go for quality over quantity, meaning that if you ensure your side hustle is the most reliable and efficient, customers will be drawn to you. There are several questions you should ask yourself when conducting market research. Before seriously thinking of what your side hustle will look like, answer the following six questions:

1. Are my interests and passions related to a certain product or service? What is it?
2. What other companies in my area offer products similar to my side hustle?
3. During my online research, have I found that many people will be interested in my product or service? Plainly put, is there a lack of this in the public space?
4. How can I be different from my competition?

5. Do I know of anyone who has been successful in a field similar to my side hustle?
6. Who would find my product or service useful? Does my side hustle only cover one demographic or a few?

The Basics of Starting a Side Hustle

When starting a side hustle, you'll need to have a business plan. A business plan isn't something you need to be worried or anxious about. In fact, it can be used to motivate you as it ensures your side hustle starts off well. A business plan doesn't have to be long, with many professionals arguing that one page is enough. When your side hustle expands and becomes a fully functional business, your business plan will undoubtedly change and include different things in response to customer feedback.

Moreover, every business plan is different and there is no perfect way to structure yours. However, there are several components that need to be included. When you construct your business plan on paper or on a laptop, be sure to add the following sections.

- **Your mission statement.** A mission statement refers to what you want your side hustle to be. For example, if you want to start a baking side hustle, your mission statement might be: "My business's mission is to provide affordable and delicious cookies to my community." You can also include some objectives directly under the statement where you state how big you want the business to be in a year or two.
- **Your target audience.** Any side hustle can be effective if you ensure that your product or service is directed at certain people. Write down who they are and state why they will be interested.

For instance, if you start a gardening business, write down that your target market consists of households with two working individuals who do not have time to keep their gardens tidy.

- **Your competition.** Every business has competition that threatens to take customers away from the owner. When you become aware of them and write them down, you can do research and find areas where they're lacking. You can then use your findings to fill the gaps where they fall short.
- **Your product or service considerations.** You should not only include what your product or service is. Add to it by writing down everything you will need to perform your side hustle efficiently. Using the earlier example of the cookie business, you'll need to write what the ingredients are, how you intend to make them, how they will be transported, and what you'll do if something happens that threatens output.
- **Your business's funding.** Money is probably the most important part of starting a side hustle. You will probably need some cash to start your business. Calculate how much you'll need to start circulation of your product or service and where you'll get it from. Once you earn an income, these financial considerations should be enhanced and become more intricate. However, your first business plan can only include your start-up costs, who will be funding you, and what your project income will be once your business is up and running.

These financial considerations are as crucial as legal considerations. You need to research what the legal framework for side hustles in your area is. There are some regions that require you to have a business license if you're working from home. Ask your family and other businesses in your area about the laws they follow. You should also consider the issue of taxes. Your age is not relevant to the amount of taxable income you make, meaning that if your income goes over a certain threshold, you'll be liable to pay business tax. You can speak to adults or maybe even make an appointment with a financial advisor who will teach you about tax returns and other legal obligations. You will also benefit from setting up a separate bank account for your business. This will help you to keep your personal and professional money separate and make tax and handling of your business finances easier.

Lean Startup Methodology

The vast majority of business startups fail in their first year. In fact, an estimated 90% of small businesses face a high risk of failure when they set up shop (Jociute, 2024). This is where the lean startup method comes into play. This methodology suggests that you develop a product or service that consumers have already shown interest in. This doesn't mean you don't look at competition, but that you identify your target market and research whether the product or service is in demand. By doing this, you'll know that there is already a market for your product, and you will definitely be successful. You can't create something and hope that demand will grow!

A big component of this methodology is the concept of a minimum viable product (MVP). This refers to an inexpensive product that meets the minimum demands of customers. When you start off with something basic, you can see how customers like it and use their feedback to adapt and improve it in the future. In other words, you gradually make your product or service more competitive as time goes on and you make higher profits. The basic lesson? Start small and perfect your product as you make more money!

Building a Brand on Social Media

Any side hustle you start needs good marketing. *Marketing* is defined as "the practice of creating interest in a product or service and convincing potential customers to buy it" (Shopify Staff, 2022). Therefore, it deals with how you advertise your product or service. In the past, business owners used television, the newspaper, and the radio to reach potential customers. In our technological age, you can make use of social media. Not only is this inexpensive, but you can reach hundreds of people in minutes.

The success of marketing depends on how consistent your brand identity is. Think about some famous businesses like McDonald's and Tesla. What do they all have in common? They are instantly recognizable, no matter where their offices are or where they choose to advertise! Your side hustle should follow the same principle.

If you create social media pages for your business across various platforms, ensure that they share your unique logo, color scheme, and messaging. You can even develop a slogan that all your pages share! Your business will be memorable when people can search for a product or service and find your various profiles on a few platforms. You also increase your chances of reaching several target markets if you are present on all of them. For example, older people are more prevalent on Facebook, whereas teens and young adults are more likely to be on TikTok and Instagram. Use all of these to market your side hustle!

However, only creating profiles is not enough for business success. You will need a *content strategy*, defined as "the planning, creation, publication, management, and governance of content" (Forsey, 2024). You should always remain interactive with your customers and post things about your business. Your posts are likely to be more successful if you inspire others to think about how beneficial your product or service will be to their lives.

Yet, building a loyal following can't be done by only posting things. You need to interact with your customers. For example, you can contact some of your customers in the comments when they praise your work and ask permission to post their reviews on your page. This will make customers feel included, while at the same time advertising how reliable you are in providing your service.

Additionally, check your pages every day and be willing to adapt them when necessary. Analyze your online profiles by looking at responses, checking how many people liked a certain post, and researching why you think a certain post wasn't as popular. These findings can be used to plan for future posts and interactions, thereby ensuring greater customer interaction. Know that you'll have to adapt and modify your content strategy as your business grows!

Balancing School and Entrepreneurship

Being an entrepreneur and starting a side hustle is surely rewarding, but you have other responsibilities as well. As you're still a teen, you'll have to balance your schoolwork with your business. Finding a place in the middle is tricky, and some teens become so overworked that they suffer from stress that ultimately decreases their performance in both of these responsibilities. You don't want to place all your attention on your side hustle and neglect schoolwork! This will jeopardize your future. There are several things you should remember when trying to balance your responsibilities.

- **Prioritization is your friend.** If you have a business while you're in school, you need to distinguish between your priorities. For example, if you have an upcoming test at school, you can't place all your attention on interacting with customers on social media. Try to make a list of all your responsibilities—your side hustle and school—and rank them from most important to least important. You can then allocate the necessary time for each responsibility based on its rank. Make use of a digital calendar by allocating separate blocks for schoolwork and business tasks. Organize them by color by making all blocks associated with school green and blocks associated with your side hustle blue, for instance. Stay true to your weekly or monthly plan and don't mix your blocks after they've been set.

- **Be realistic about your goals.** As it's impossible to place all your attention on your side hustle while you're in school, be realistic about your business goals. Don't expect to become an industry leader as a teen. Remember your side hustle is also a learning experience. Your highest goals should be kept for school because your education is what will always carry you through. Given the changing nature of the business world, your goals for your side hustle should start off small and gradually become larger. If you're not successful at first, don't sweat it! You have a lot of time to perfect your side hustle.
- **Manage your time.** This is related to prioritization but includes other factors. Namely, focus on one thing at a time. If you've set aside time to work on your side hustle, don't think about your schoolwork. All your attention should be placed on what you're currently busy with. Think about the times of the day when you're most productive and split these between your business and work responsibilities. For example, if you know you're most productive in the evening, set aside two hours to work on your side hustle on an evening you know you won't

have homework. Similarly, when you're at school or busy with a school project, forget about your side hustle temporarily. When you have allocated time for each, you won't feel as though you're neglecting either.

It's expected that you'll occasionally have a difficult time balancing your side hustle and school. If you do, know that there is help! Your family and friends are great sources of encouragement and support. If you feel like you're doing too much, talk to your loved ones and ask if they have advice on how you can prioritize better or manage your time more efficiently. You can also speak to a teacher or your school counselor. They will certainly give you some helpful tips on what you can do when everything seems too much. Remember that you're a teen and still deserve to have some fun in your free time. Even if your side hustle is your passion, it still tires you and draws mental and physical energy. Never be ashamed of having to take some downtime and do nothing. Everyone needs to recuperate and relax from time to time.

Now that you know how to start a side hustle, you can make a decision on whether it's for you. If you think that a part-time job with a dependable income is better for you, you can prepare for the job market. For this, you need an impressive resume and interview skills. You will learn all about this in the next chapter!

Key Takeaways

- A *side hustle* is defined as, "A flexible job that you work at 'to the side' of your primary job" (Team Everlance, 2022). Because you're probably still in school, a side hustle refers to anything you do in your spare time that exercises your entrepreneurial spirit.

- Before starting a side hustle, you should identify your entrepreneurial interests. You should remember three things when doing this: Ask yourself what you're curious about, don't make money your primary goal, and don't be afraid to change course. Market research is also very important and tasks you with researching your prospective clientele.
- Any side hustle requires a business plan. There are several things to be outlined in the plan, including your mission statement, your target audience, your competition, your product and service considerations, and your business's funding.
- It's helpful to use the *lean startup methodology* when starting a side hustle. This refers to developing a product or service people have already shown interest in. *Minimum viable product* (MVP) is related to this methodology and involves initially creating an inexpensive product that meets the minimum demands of customers.
- Marketing your side hustle is crucial for success. You can use social media to advertise your product or service on various online platforms. The most crucial component in doing this is ensuring your business has a consistent brand identity wherever it's advertised.
- You will need to balance your schoolwork and business if you start your side hustle. In order to strike this balance, you should prioritize, be realistic about your goals, and manage your time.

CHAPTER 8:

Preparing for the Job Market

By failing to prepare, you're preparing to fail. –Benjamin Franklin

PREPARING FOR THE JOB MARKET IS CERTAINLY intimidating! When you start school, everything is laid out for you on your path. You know what you're expected to do and what your near future looks like. Finding work is completely different. Your success depends on you and the choices you make.

As discussed earlier, there are thousands of employers, and all have unique ways of hiring prospective employees. You can't expect to know how you'll be perceived by employers and recruiters. However, you can be as prepared as possible. There are two crucial components in your work preparation toolkit: Your resume and your interview skills. When these are accounted for and done well, you are much more likely to find the job that's right for you. One expert wrote, "[A good resume] can make the difference between landing an interview and being overlooked" (Bothra, 2023). In the case that you land an interview, an impeccable performance is the final hurdle toward employment. Let's look at how you can craft a standout resume first!

Crafting a Standout Resume

One study found that recruiters only spend about seven seconds looking at a resume before deciding whether they're interested in the applicant (Ladder Inc, 2018). As you're not the only person applying for a position, your resume needs to stand out from the crowd.

You only have a brief window to impress recruiters and employers! You will benefit from keeping your resume to one page. Employers generally don't want to spend a lot of time reading your resume—that is what the interview is for. All they want is a short, simple introduction to who you are so that they can see if you meet the requirements. Your resume is merely a tool you use to get your foot in the door so that you can impress the employer when going for an interview. Your resume should have a professional format whereby all your various lists are clearly labeled in a professional font like Arial or Times New Roman. When you're writing your resume, ensure that you have the following:

- **Your stats:** Any resume should be prefaced with your name, your LinkedIn profile, email address, and phone number. You can decide if you want to add a photograph, but this is not always necessary. Should you want to include a photograph of you, make sure that it looks professional behind a clear backdrop.
- **A short introduction:** Under your stats, you should include four or five sentences about yourself. Here, you can stress what kind of person you are and why you're interested in the job you're applying for. This section benefits from having some

soft skills. For example, you can emphasize your leadership, problem-solving, and teamwork skills. When an employer reads this, they should be impressed by your favorable attributes.

- **Your education and experience:** Quantifying is the rule in this section. This means that you write the dates of your involvement with your school or experience next to the name. You can include volunteering or any summer job in this section and structure them in bullet points. For example, one bullet point might say "June 2023 to August 2023: Volunteered at Habitat for Humanity." Your bullet point list should be chronological beginning with the earliest start date to the most current one.
- **Your hard and soft skills:** When your education and experience have been highlighted, create a list of your skills. Your hard skills refer to your technical abilities like being able to speak another language. On the other hand, your soft skills—although some were mentioned in the introduction—should be expanded on. List your soft skills by stating you are adaptable and creative, for example.
- **Any activities or hobbies:** End your resume by listing anything you enjoy doing. This will give the employer a better idea of who you are. You can write that you like reading, hiking, or cooking, for example. It doesn't necessarily have to deal with the job you're applying for. However, if you recognize that a particular interest relates to your job application, you should definitely add it!
- **Your references:** The bottom of your resume should always include a few names and phone numbers of people you've worked for. If you have only volunteered or taken part in school activities, you can add the names of the charity

organizers or your teachers. Note that you should always check with the person whether you can use them as a reference! If they agree, add their name, role, and phone number. This way, the employer can give them a call and check whether your resume is valid and truthful.

Tailoring Your Resume

You must never send the same resume to all positions you're applying for. Your resume is supposed to be a changing document, but this doesn't mean you should write a new resume for every job. You can use your basic resume and modify it to suit the job you're applying for.

Before planning to send your resume, read the job description for the particular posting a few times. Oftentimes, the employer will use keywords and phrases as they relate to the nature of the job. After reading this, compare your resume and look where you can add these keywords. Ask yourself: *Did the employer list certain skills? What soft skills are they looking for?* Use this to guide you in updating your resume.

Add certain skills—that you know you have—to your resume that associate with the job description. Moreover, highlight any experience or school subjects under the education and experience sections that relate to the job. Proofread the changes you made to your resume and imagine yourself as the employer or recruiter reading about you. Will they be impressed? Do your skills correlate to what they're looking for? Is your experience beneficial to the role? Remember to go through your updated resume a few times and check for spelling and grammar mistakes. Every employer should get a unique and spotless resume!

The Art of Writing Cover Letters

Accompanying your resume is your cover letter. A cover letter is a short introduction of yourself to the employer, usually consisting of between 250 and 400 words. The aim of a cover letter is to convince the employer that you're the right person for the job. A resume is essentially a list of what you've done and what skills you have. Therefore, it doesn't necessarily indicate what kind of person you are.

A cover letter fills in those gaps and allows the employer to get to know you personally through your written words. Of course, not everyone is a great writer, but if you write a cover letter from the heart, your possible employer will surely want to meet you! There's no such thing as the perfect cover letter as everyone is unique. Yet, most consist of three main paragraphs or sections. By following five guidelines you'll be able to write an impressive cover letter!

1. **Cover the basics.** Like your resume, the header of your cover letter should have all your information. Namely, your name, email address, phone number, and LinkedIn profile. The date must also be included, and the particulars of the recipient should be added. You can ask a family member or teacher to help you with the specifics regarding how you should structure the recipient's details, like the company name.
2. **Open with a professional greeting.** After the basics have been covered, you can address the recipient—the recruiter or employer. It's always best to start with "Dear [first and last name]" (Herrity, 2024b). Other forms of greetings like "To whom it may concern" seem pretentious and impersonal. You want the reader to think you're friendly, while at the same time professional.

3. **The first section.** Begin this section by clearly stating what role you're applying for and why you chose the specific company. Convey your interest in the company by telling them what you found in your research. If the company is one of the biggest employers in your area, for example, explain that you admire what they mean to the community. You should include why the company is great, and that it would be an honor to work for them. The purpose of this paragraph is to show the employer you specifically chose their company and this specific role because it's one of the best!

4. **The second section.** Once you've explained why you chose their company, go into your second paragraph that surrounds your background and experience. The goal is to tell them about your education or career journey as it pertains to the role you're applying for. Focus on your experience that relates to the job you're applying for. For example, if you're applying for a part-time job at a kindergarten, explain that you have volunteered at a children's home. Note that this should be completely truthful, and you can't ever lie about your experience. Explain how your experience, even if it's not expansive, will benefit you in the role you're applying for and how you'll benefit the company.

5. **The third section.** This section will deal with your skills and values as it relates to the job description. Tell the employer about your soft skills and how they can be used in the role you want to interview for. As your skills are outlined in your resume, you can highlight two or three that are most important for the job. You can give two or three real-life examples where you used these skills so that they have evidence for your claims. It's recommended to end the cover letter by bringing the topic back to the company's mission statement and explaining how your skills and values align with the company's objectives.

Should I Customize My Cover Letter?

It's not recommended that you simply customize or modify your cover letter in the same way you would your resume. A new cover letter should be written for every job you apply for. Not only do you address different recruiters or employers personally, but each job description is completely unique. Each cover letter must account for the specific role and company you're applying to. Sure, this will make more work for you, but it's necessary if you want to make a lasting impression on every company you apply to. If you get stuck and you're not certain what to write about, you can look for online tools that provide cover letter and resume templates. A great website is Canva. You can search for templates and use them as guidance when constructing both your resume and cover letters!

An Effective Job Searching Strategy

With your resume and cover letter under your belt, you can start your job search. As has been mentioned before, if you don't have a LinkedIn profile, you're essentially nonexistent in the modern workplace! If you don't already have a LinkedIn profile, create one as soon as possible. Once you have a profile, you can go to your settings, turn on notifications, and give LinkedIn the right to email you when a job in your career field opens up. Having this activated allows you to apply immediately when an employer posts a job opening. Before you do this, check that you have chosen several companies or job titles so that you get the correct notifications!

However, you don't need to wait for alerts. You can actively search for job postings by entering a few keywords. If you're looking for a short-term job in the food industry, use keywords like "kitchen" and "restaurant." This will open up dozens of opportunities in the location you choose. When you've identified a few opportunities you'd like to interview for, save them and start working on modifying your resume and writing cover letters. Read the poster's profile and see what the company is all about, using what you learn to guide your cover letter.

While you're looking, you'll frequently see the option of filling out an application. Oftentimes, the opening doesn't require a resume and only asks you to submit an online application. It's suggested that you do this in addition to uploading your resume. There are no downsides to giving a prospective employer a resume, while also uploading an application. You will look determined and won't run the risk of having your application get lost in the pool of other submissions. You can also add your basic resume to your LinkedIn profile which will allow recruiters to read about you when looking for candidates for a position in your career field.

Although this resume isn't targeted toward a specific company, it will indicate the field you work in and the experience you have. When a recruiter contacts you, you can modify the uploaded resume to suit a specific company's needs and send it to them.

Most importantly, don't lose hope or refrain from checking in regularly. You might not find something quickly or even see a posting that appeals to you, but the speed at which new jobs are posted makes up for it! Visit LinkedIn regularly and look at the various opportunities that are uploaded daily.

Preparing for Job Interviews

When you get a call or email confirming your application has been successful, the only thing left to do is the interview. Getting invited for an interview means that your resume and cover letter were impressive, and you've aced the first step! Now, you carry all the responsibility to convince the interviewer you're right for the job. Your interview will probably take place in person, but you might start off with a preliminary phone or video call.

In both of these cases, it's essential that you read the job description again and do some research on the company you're interviewing for. Write down any facts you find and memorize them before the interview. The interviewer will be excited about your knowledge of the company. You should also make sure that you're on time. There's nothing worse than making an interviewer wait! Be early and prepared for them when they want to start speaking with you.

It's also beneficial to have another resume handy that you can give to the interviewer in person or look at when you're interviewing over the phone. This will help you give true details and speak with passion. Always be respectful of the interviewer and use positive body language in person or over a video call. When the interview is finished, send them a thank-you email to show your appreciation.

The STAR Method

All interviews consist of a series of *behavioral interview questions*, defined as "questions or statements that ask job candidates to share examples of specific situations they've been in" (Zhang, 2023). The reason is that your resume has already proven you can do the job. All the interviewer wants to know is whether you have the soft skills to fit in and advance the company's unique work environment. Simply put, they want to see if you're the right fit! You won't know exactly what they'll be asking, but you can practice the basics of how you intend to answer these hypothetical questions about your responses to certain situations.

This is where the STAR method comes in. STAR consists of four steps in successfully answering a question, ensuring that you leave a lasting impression on an interviewer. It can be applied to any behavioral or situational prompt, but by looking at a typical interview question, you can see how it works. Let's look at the steps and how they can be applied to the following question: "Tell me about a time you faced a work-related problem. How did you solve it?"

- **Situation:** The first step in answering the question should be to provide context, meaning you tell the interviewer the story behind the problem. It's best to keep the context short and only highlight the most important aspects. Using the question above, your context will be: "When I submitted a project for school, my teacher told me I misunderstood the task, and that I should do it again. She gave me time to correct it."
- **Task:** Follow the situation by telling the interviewer about the task you had. This means you note your responsibility in the situation, and what you should have done to fix it. Ask yourself: How did I have to deal with the situation? For example, "I had three days to develop a fresh project, by doing more research and ensuring I give it my best."
- **Action:** This is the part of your answer that will probably be the longest. In the action step, you explain how you fixed the problem to ensure the best result. Here, it's crucial that you use "I" regularly to show that you take responsibility for your actions. For example, "I managed my time during the three days so that I had four hours to work on the project. I went to the library and found several articles I could use to add to the project's content. I also spoke to some of my teachers for advice."
- **Result:** In this step, you talk about what your actions led to and how they were enough to rectify the situation. You want the interviewer to feel confident that you treated the situation as a learning opportunity and grew as a result. For example,

"All my efforts impressed my teacher, and I got an A plus for the project. I learned that I'm able to do anything if I set my mind to it and hard work always pays off. I also learned effective time management and how to use constructive criticism as a tool to make a better product."

By following this technique, all your answers can be impressive and flawless! Going for interviews is a learning process and you might make a few mistakes when going for your first one. It's normal to get nervous. However, you can practice your answers by having mock interviews with family or friends.

Do some research online and look for articles that detail common interview questions. Print them out and give it to your loved one so that you can practice your answers. When they ask you something, use the STAR method to answer and ask what they thought about your response. Maybe you have to tweak something or modify your responses until they think you're ready.

Nonetheless, when you're in a real interview, your ability to *ask* questions is similarly important. Write down some questions you have for the interviewer and ask them when the interview allows you to. When you do this, it demonstrates your interest and desire to work with them. Ask questions like, what do you look for in an employee? And what kind of workplace culture do you promote? The interviewer will see you as an inquisitive person who is very serious about the job!

Creating your first resume and cover letter and going for an interview is exciting! You'll learn more about yourself and become better as a result. Yet, you shouldn't expect that you won't make any mistakes. Life is too complicated! In the next chapter, you'll learn how to face failure and build resilience!

Key Takeaways

- A resume, preferably one page long, is essential in your job search. Your resume should include your stats, a short personal introduction, your education and experience, your hard and soft skills, any personal activities and hobbies, and your references.
- Your cover letter, a document telling the employer more about you, should accompany your resume. Your cover letter must include your basic information, followed by a professional greeting. It should then be broken down into three paragraphs or sections. The first dealing with your interest in the job, the second dealing with your background and experience, and the third dealing with your skills and values.
- Finding work on LinkedIn can be daunting. There are several things you can do to maximize your job search. They include turning notifications on so that you're alerted about a new posting, using keywords related to your desired job in the search box, sending a modified resume to each job—even if you can fill in an online application—and checking the website regularly.
- During interviews, the interviewer will ask you a series of behavioral interview questions to estimate how you'll act in work-related situations. You can practice your ability to answer by using the STAR method. Answer any question by first providing the context—or situation—in which the problem arose, then clarifying the task you had, followed by what your actions were in solving it, and ending by noting what the favorable result was.

Online Resources

- **Canva:** https://www.canva.com/
- **LinkedIn:** https://www.linkedin.com/

CHAPTER 9:

Facing Failure and Building Resilience

There is no failure except in no longer trying. –Chris Bradford

WHAT DO YOU THINK WALT DISNEY, THE FOUNDER OF the Disney company, Colonel Sanders, the founder of Kentucky Fried Chicken (KFC), and J.K. Rowling, the author of the Harry Potter series, had in common? They all encountered failure! Walt Disney lost his job at the *Kansas City Star* newspaper as a young man because his boss told him he "lacked imagination and had no good ideas" (Johnson, 2023). Colonel Sanders was rejected by 1,009 restaurants because his chicken recipe was supposedly not tasty enough (Nafte, 2017). And J.K. Rowling's first Harry Potter book was rejected by 12 publishing houses! (Millington, 2018).

However, they did not let these setbacks stop them. Each of them used their failure as a source of motivation and practiced resilience in the face of temporary adversity. Later in life they would all look back on their alleged "failures" and realize that they got through it and were abundantly rewarded as a result. Like them, you can also get through any career obstacle or disappointment. Of course, you will fail sometimes, but you have the choice to embrace it or not. When you cultivate a resilient mindset, your career journey will always end up being a success. Let's learn how you can transform your understanding of failure first!

Understanding Failure as a Learning Tool

Ask anyone and they'll tell you that failure doesn't feel good. Whether you weren't successful in a school exam or weren't invited for an interview after sending your resume, it hurts! Nevertheless, if you reframe your thinking about failure, you'll learn that it can be a blessing in disguise. When you're not successful in something, you're given the gift of trying again and bettering yourself. Failure is a learning tool and can be viewed as the primary ingredient that pushes you toward a brighter future. There are a few things you should understand in order to reframe your negative association with failure.

- **Employ the concept of "failing forward."** When you aren't successful in something, you shouldn't focus on the failure itself. Rather, think of the reasons as to why your actions or efforts fell short. Use the negative experience to build a new strategy that is more likely to yield the result you want. For example, if you were not hired after an interview for a summer job, gather extra interview questions from the internet and have more mock interviews with your family and friends. Therefore, you won't be damaged by what happened because you'll be too busy working on a new—more successful—plan. You'll surely bounce back with everything you learn.

- **Don't link yourself to the failure.** When your efforts fall short, you're inclined to think that you're a failure or that you're not good enough. This is wrong! When you don't succeed on your first try, it has nothing to do with you as a person. A temporary failure is not part of your identity. If something negative happens, tell yourself: *This is not an indication of who I am.* Moreover, there is no shame in occasionally failing. How boring would life be if you never made a mistake? As basketball player Michael Jordan said, "I've failed over and over and over again in my life, and that is why I succeed" (Taj, 2019).
- **Find purpose in your failure.** Nothing difficult you go through is meaningless. Life is too short to complain when something doesn't go as planned. If you fail, think of the reasons why and what you can do to fix it. If you face failure and work on a solution, you're bound to enjoy your successes even more. You can even create a failure resume, meaning a document in which you list any occasion where you failed and add the lessons you learned from it. For example, if you had an argument with one of your volunteering colleagues, you could write it down and explain that you learned not to aggravate a professional conversation by yelling. Your failures always provide insight regarding what you can do to build a better future!

Analyzing Your Failures

On the occasion that you failed or made a mistake, don't sit for hours and think of yourself negatively. A much better solution is to analyze your failure and learn from it immediately. That way, you can face it quickly and work on yourself as soon as it happens. There are five optimistic questions you can ask yourself in the aftermath of failure.

1. What was my role in contributing to the negative outcome?
2. What are three things this failure taught me about myself?
3. What could I have done differently?
4. What personal or professional skills can I work on to ensure something similar doesn't happen again?
5. Who can help me overcome this failure and help me in becoming better?

Building Resilience

Resilience is defined as "the ability to withstand adversity and bounce back from difficult life events" (Hurley, 2024). If you've found that you're able to recover quickly with a high level of motivation, you're a resilient person! However, resilience doesn't always come naturally. You have to work on it and encounter failure in order to build it. Disappointment or difficulties will definitely arise as you march forward in your career path, but if you're resilient, you can get through them and come out stronger on the other end. Building resilience takes time and is unique to every individual, but there are some things you can do if you need to work on it.

1. **The first thing is to deal with your emotions properly.** If you fail, your first instinct is to become angry or sad. This is where self-care comes in. Of course, you'll have negative emotions when met with problems, but if you practice calming techniques regularly, you'll approach your failures more effectively. By being more mindful during the course of the day—meaning you slow down and relax through slow breathing—you'll be able to cope effectively.

2. **The second is to make a positive decision when you've failed.** You might be inclined to obsess over your mistake, but this won't make anything better. Rather, tell yourself that the difficulty was only a hurdle, and you can get through it. Perspective is important as well, in that any failure is a tiny part of your life! Reframe your negative experience by comparing it to the vastness of your life. The situation might seem overwhelming in the moment, but when you're old one day, you will not even remember it.

3. **The third is to be more confident in your abilities.** Self-confidence is the best ingredient for resilience! After a failure, think of all the positive things you've done and remind yourself of all your good qualities. Ask yourself: *What are four things I'm good at? And what do people usually compliment me for?* By filling your mind with all your favorable traits, you'll find that any failure is only a bump in the road. You're much more than any negative scenario!

4. **The fourth is to lean on your family and friends.** You can get through anything if you're surrounded by people you love. You can overcome stress and cope with all failures if you have a strong support system that'll be there for you no matter what. Although you might not be successful in something, your loved ones will make you feel cared for and reduce feelings of isolation. For example, if you didn't land the part-time job you desperately wanted, you'll know that you have a home where you'll always belong. Speak to your family and friends when you've failed. They'll encourage you and maybe provide you with some tips on how to learn from your mistakes.

Challenge Yourself!

As mentioned earlier, your resilience is only built when met with challenges. The key is to face some challenges before serious problems come your way. You can do this by actively searching for different challenges available to you. This might seem confusing because no one likes to make mistakes! Yet, the good thing is that a small challenge while you're a teen won't carry lasting effects. Embrace challenges by trying new activities you find difficult at first. For example, sign up for the debate club if you're scared of speaking in front of people. Start doing a sport you're not confident about, or volunteer for an organization that seems daunting. As you force yourself to face your fears, you might make a mistake, but you'll learn how to depend on yourself. These experiences will teach you many lessons and make you more resilient!

The Power of a Growth Mindset

Overcoming failure by being more resilient depends on your decision to foster a growth mindset as opposed to a fixed mindset. A *growth mindset* refers to "an internal belief that [your] talents and intelligence can be developed through hard work, dedication, and a willingness to learn" (Ryan, 2024).

On the flip side, a *fixed mindset* refers to the belief that all your abilities are innate—or inborn—and can't be developed or changed. By merely looking at the many skills you developed during your school career, you can clearly see that a growth mindset is the right way to go!

Having a growth or fixed mindset is a choice. Imagine you get a good grade for an exam. If you have a fixed mindset, you'll tell yourself that you must be very intelligent. However, if you have a growth mindset, you'll tell yourself that you worked hard, and your studying strategies paid off. In other words, a growth mindset permits you to give yourself and your efforts more credit. It also makes you recognize that your future is in your hands and that you can achieve anything if you put your mind to it. It's important to remember that building a growth mindset takes time and requires you to make consistent decisions when experiencing new things that threaten your confidence. There are several things you can do.

One is to focus more on the process than the result. Even if you weren't successful in a certain endeavor, the process you went through definitely taught you new things. For instance, if you went for an interview but didn't get the job, you should analyze what you learned during the interview and how these lessons can be used in your next interview. Therefore, you don't harp on the fact that you didn't get the job, but you celebrate that you went for an interview and are more prepared for the next one.

You should also view any challenge as an opportunity, as opposed to a difficulty. When first hearing about something you need to do, don't immediately jump to what could go wrong. Instead, think about what the experience will teach you, even if you don't achieve the desirable result. Additionally, be open to experimentation! This means that you confront challenges with different approaches and gain insight into why or why it didn't work. Simply put, don't aim for perfection, but aim for better than before. Be proud of yourself when you try something new and don't succeed the first time around. Remember to share your experiences with your loved ones and ask them for advice. They'll always be proud of you no matter what!

Handling Rejection With Grace

You always benefit from constructive criticism. When your teacher, parent, or prospective employer gives you feedback about a lack in your performance, think about what they said and how you can work on it. Known as the feedback loop, receive what they said with an open mind and work on solutions to solve the problem and become better. However, what do you do if you try your best and you're rejected?

Not getting the job you wanted can be very hurtful. Sometimes, you'll send your resume or even go for an interview, only to hear nothing back from them. This is all too common and is the reason why some online workplaces recommend job seekers send their resumes to no less than 10 companies a week (Indeed Editorial Team, 2023)! When met with rejection, reframe it to redirection. This means that you accept the situation and use the experience to motivate you to change your approach or change course. If you're rejected, you can get through it by employing the following steps.

1. **Be kind to yourself.** If you face rejection, it will hurt. Don't be too hard on yourself! It's expected that you'll need a few moments—or a period of time—to work through it. Constantly remind yourself that there's nothing wrong with you, but that things are how they should be. If you didn't get a specific job, for example, it simply wasn't meant for you.
2. **Take pride in yourself.** If you get rejected, it means you put yourself out there and were confident enough to trust your abilities. Rather than stressing the fact that you didn't meet your goal, take comfort in your willingness to take risks. People who lack confidence never put themselves in positions where they can be rejected. You're not one of them! Know that you tried your best and that this obstacle will only make you more motivated.

3. **Remove yourself from the rejection.** It's okay to spend a small amount of time sulking about not getting something you really wanted. However, don't do this for more than a day. It's not suggested that you forget the experience immediately, but you should avoid letting the situation define you. Don't play the situation out in your mind several times and beat yourself up with negative self-talk. This will only harm your self-esteem.
4. **Search for the lesson.** Every time you get rejected, you're gifted the ability to learn something new about yourself or your desired career. Think about the positives and what you can do to avoid something similar from happening in the future. Maybe your resume needs tweaking, maybe you should practice positive body language more, or maybe you need to look at a different field of work completely. When you don't mean a goal, always ask yourself: *What is this teaching me?*

Although rejection is painful, you should always remain professional. Never take it personally—it's just business after all. If a prospective employer contacts you to let you know that you didn't make the cut, be respectful and thank them for the opportunity. The more respectable you are, the more likely they are to remember you. Moreover, don't be afraid of sending a follow-up email or phone call, especially if you sent your resume and have not heard back. Your persistence and determination will always be viewed as favorable attributes, even if they don't want to work with you.

As you've read in earlier chapters, networking is crucial in the world of work. Sometimes, you might not get the job you want, but the employer, interviewer, or hopeful colleague will remember you if you remain kind and professional. Maybe they'll invite you back if another job opens up! Most importantly, use the rejection to pivot to bigger and greater things. After you've accepted the rejection, work on new ways to put yourself out there and search for other opportunities that match your career goals.

Once you're capable of facing any failures through tapping into your resilience, you're on the right path. Your strength and determination will carry you toward a bright future. Now that you know how to do this, you're ready to take the necessary steps toward your career aspirations. In the next chapter, you'll be learning about that!

Key Takeaways

- Failure is something that everyone experiences during their lifetimes and in their careers. The key is to understand failure as a learning tool. You do this by employing the concept of "failing forward," not linking yourself to your failure, and finding purpose in your failure. When you analyze your mistake, you can learn lessons from it.
- You need resilience if you want to succeed in your career. *Resilience* is defined as "the ability to withstand adversity and bounce back from difficult life events" (Hurley, 2024). You can build it by dealing with your emotions, making positive decisions after you fail, being more confident in your abilities, and leaning on family and friends.
- You can also build resilience by challenging yourself as a teen. Try to do things that scare you. For example, if you're shy, sign up for the debate club and be open to making mistakes there. The more challenging experiences you go through, the better able you are to bounce back from more serious failures.
- You should aim to foster a growth mindset as opposed to a fixed mindset. A *growth mindset* refers to "an internal belief that

[your] talents and intelligence can be developed through hard work, dedication, and a willingness to learn" (Ryan, 2024). You do this by focusing more on the process than on the result, experimenting with different things, and celebrating any small achievement you have.

- Rejection is a part of your career path. When you're rejected by a prospective employer and don't land the job you want, there are a few things you can do. Namely, be kind to yourself, take pride in yourself, remove yourself from rejection, and search for the lessons you learned.

CHAPTER 10:

Your Future Starts Now!

It is not in the stars to hold our destiny but in ourselves. –William Shakespeare

ANYTHING NEW YOU DO IN YOUR LIFE TASKS YOU with taking the first step. Think back to your first day in high school. It seemed daunting and scary at first, but as you took the leap and gradually became accustomed to it, the easier it got. The same is true for your career path.

Your future career is still relatively unknown, and you don't really know what to expect. You're going to experience new things and learn more about yourself, and you'll certainly face difficulties that will show you the complexities of adult life. Sure, this can make you a bit anxious, but you can do it! Any step toward a brighter future and a thriving career is never done in vain, and you can start the journey toward your career dreams right now. Your adventure is undoubtedly going to be unique, challenging, and exhilarating all at the same time. All you need to do is to trust yourself. Always remember that you're worthy of everything you want to achieve!

Taking the First Step

One of the biggest hurdles you'll need to overcome when preparing to take your first step is fear of the unknown. Also described as the "one fear to rule them all," not knowing what will happen can create a big obstacle prior to embarking on your career path (Pratt, 2024). This fear can make you avoid starting. It's a normal occurrence, but you can get through it!

Oftentimes, this is associated with a fear of failure as you don't know if your career steps will be successful. The only solution to resisting this avoidance tactic is to think about the deeper causes of your fear. Ask yourself: *What am I afraid of? Why is it scary? And what's the worst that can happen?* When you analyze the possible outcomes, you'll find that the worst result isn't even that bad. The worst thing that can happen is that you won't get the job you want. Is that the end of the world? The answer is no!

Embrace the fear and accept it as part of your journey. That is the only way you'll put your foot in the door. You should avoid falling into a *state of inertia*, defined as "The tendency to maintain the status quo [through inaction]" (A, 2021). Simply put, when you prefer to stay in your comfort zone.

The truth is that staying in your comfort zone won't push you toward your career aspirations. You need to force yourself to get out there, which is made easier if you start off by taking very small steps. Don't set a goal of immediately finding a job. You should rather set a smaller goal, such as working on your resume first. Once that step is complete, take another small step, such as researching career options. When you become acclimatized to your career aspirations slowly, you'll gradually build yourself up to embrace bigger challenges.

Remember that the smallest step is already an accomplishment and encourages your eventual realization of your career goals. Any step you take—no matter how small—creates a ripple effect of success. Using the earlier example, making a CV will motivate you to put the document to work by creating a LinkedIn profile. This will open new opportunities and prove that you're worthy of reaching your bright future. Sometimes, a small step can open entirely new doors as well. If you urge yourself to take the step by speaking to a family member currently working in a career you aspire to, they might speak to their company and organize something for you. The basic rule? Take any step toward your goals and build on that.

Continuous Learning and Skill Development

Once you've taken your first step, you'll be encouraged to continue your preparation for greater things. Continuous preparation is a prerequisite for success in any career. When you stay in a constant state of learning, you'll have more confidence in yourself to search for more opportunities and subsequently become more attractive to prospective employers.

One way in which you can do this is by keeping an eye on emerging skills in your desired career field. You can learn more about your hopeful career online and search for opportunities to do so. Research your hopeful career and see what you can do now to develop the skills you'll need. Helpful tools include webinars, online job platforms, and industry-specific podcasts. You can also look for free online courses you could do in your free time. One website that offers this is Massive Open Online Courses (MOOC). There, you'll find courses that don't cost you anything, but give you an upper hand as you climb your career ladder.

Creating a Personal Development Plan

You will similarly benefit from creating a personal development plan. This type of plan differs from your career plan because it stresses how you can develop yourself more comprehensively. Your personal development plan should be short and concise so that you can take a quick look at it when you need some encouragement and guidance. The main point of your plan should deal with skill development—skills that will help you make your career goals a reality. There are several things that should be included in this plan.

- **Your particular area of development:** This is the skill you want to work on. For example, if you want to be a better communicator, this will be added here.
- **Your primary objective:** In this section, you'll need to define what your ultimate goal is after doing all the personal work in accordance with your stated area of development. For example, your objective can be, "I want to be able to lead a team effectively."
- **Your behavioral changes:** Here, you need to write what you'll work on personally to make your objective more likely. For example, you can indicate that you'll practice calming techniques when in conversation with a group.
- **Your actions toward your objective:** Whereas your behavioral changes deal with how you want to prepare in a personal capacity, your actions are things you need to do that deal specifically with your goal. For example, you can clarify

that you'll ask if you can lead a team on your next group project in school.

- **Your date of completion:** You're more likely to meet your goals if you set a time when you want it to be finished. For example, you can tell yourself that you want to reach your objective in three months. This will keep your actions toward your goal in a timeframe, making it likelier that you'll reach it.

Documenting Your Journey

American author Carolyn Hamilton wrote, "Documenting little details of your everyday life becomes a celebration of who you are" (Barry, 2018). If you're on social media and post pictures of yourself and your adventures, you're documenting your life. This begs the question: Why won't you do the same with your career path? Your career path is something you should be proud of and reflect on as you advance it. When you document everything that happens—whether that be building a skill or going for an interview—you'll appreciate all the efforts you've made in making your bright future a reality.

When all your instances of success are recorded, you'll not only have something to go to when your confidence takes an unexpected blow but you'll be motivated to go forward. You might not think that something you do is a big deal, but if you look at everything in hindsight, you'll find that all your small steps accumulated and resulted in where you are today. Keeping note of all your developed skills and experiences is also important when you look for work because it assists you in building your resume or preparing for an interview. Documenting your journey doesn't take a lot of time if you write it down whenever you achieve something small.

The best way to do this is by keeping a professional journal. This can either be done on your computer or in a physical journal. You might prefer keeping an online document, but some professionals argue that writing in a physical journal is more promising. In fact, research has found that when you write in a journal, your brain is more active (Tabac, 2021).

Documenting your career journey in a journal allows you to keep track of everything, while also encouraging you to write your feelings surrounding it. In other words, you can write a particular achievement while also noting how it made you feel about yourself. This enhances your capacity for reflection and makes you see just how far you've come! Your professional journal will give you a glimpse into what you've done and all the steps you've taken to reach your dreams. When something negative happens, you'll always have your positive thoughts and successes stored in a special document, allowing you to read it to find solace and greater resilience. Remembering that you've gone through difficult times makes a temporary failure bearable. You can do anything if you set your mind to it, and your professional journal will prove this time and time again!

Key Takeaways

- In starting your career path, you'll need to take the first step. This can be difficult because you might have a fear of the unknown. You can overcome this by embracing the fear and accepting it as part of your journey.
- You should also avoid falling into a *state of inertia*, defined as "the tendency to maintain the status quo [through inaction]" (A, 2021). You can do this by taking very small, actionable

steps that slowly bring you toward your goals without causing intense anxiety or worry.

- You can foster a sense of continuous learning and skill development by keeping track of changes in your career field and using various tools—like MOOC—to build on your skills and motivation.
- A personal development plan can help you in your path toward your aspired career. This differs from a career plan because it focuses more on your personal growth. In developing a personal development plan, you should add the following: Your particular area of development, your primary objectives, your behavioral changes, your actions toward your objective, and a date of completion.
- Documenting your career journey is very important. You can either write all your successes, experiences, and skill-building ventures on a digital document or in a professional journal. It's recommended that you have a physical journal.

Online Resources

- **MOOC:** https://www.mooc.org/

CONCLUSION

"LUCK IS WHAT HAPPENS WHEN PREPARATION MEETS opportunity" (Frasier, 2016). This age-old advice first written by the ancient philosopher, Seneca, remains true. Luck is not something that just happens randomly! It only arrives when you prepare effectively and grasp all opportunities that are available to you. Your career is something you need to work on now!

Before reading this book, you might have believed that your career is still far in the future and that you don't really need to think about it before you graduate. You've found that this thinking is flawed! Your career is your responsibility, and you can use all the tools at your disposal to make your bright future a reality. The options are endless and you're lucky to live in the time you are, with new industries, technologies, and opportunities for skill-building scattered all around you. You can replace your apprehension with excitement because you have the ability to construct a future beyond your wildest dreams. All you need to do is find what works for you and have the determination to carry on until you reach your goals. The bottom line? You can begin crafting your career while you're a teen and be rewarded with a successful life.

In this book, you have discovered techniques you can use to discover what you really want in a career. Your passions, strengths, and values were uncovered, and you probably have a better idea of what kind of work will fit your personality well.

By learning what the world of work looks like today, you're in the position of mapping your career path through setting SMART goals, adjusting your plans regarding your education once you're finished with school, and constructing a career action plan. Not only that, but you know how to develop key skills that will prove beneficial to any career you choose.

As you worked on your critical thinking, problem-solving, communication, teamwork, and leadership skills, you've ensured that any prospective employer will be lucky to have you on the payroll! You also know what you can do to gain real-world experience through applying for an internship or volunteering. Maybe you're impressed by how impactful a simple summer job can be to add to your professional experience. The importance of networking and mentorship was not overlooked, and you have the basics on how you can use these essential endeavors in advancing your career.

By either starting a side hustle—where you exercise your entrepreneurial skills—or preparing for the job market, you are prepared for the future. Because you learned how to create an outstanding resume and cover letter, your chances of landing an interview are more than probable.

Similarly, you know how to prepare for an interview and impress prospective employers as you use the STAR method to answer any question like a true professional. You have never been in a better position to find your dream career than you are now! As you encounter failure, you'll learn from it and become a more resilient person who will carry you throughout your life.

Use everything you learned in this book to guide you and take charge of your future! It's never too early, and when you apply the teachings of this book—in addition to using the many online resources made available—you'll succeed in anything you take on. Keep these lessons close to you and read chapters again when you need some help. If you stick to this approach, you can't fail. So, what's stopping you? Go make your dream career a reality!

Thank you for reading! If you enjoyed this book, we'd really appreciate it if you could leave a review on Amazon. This will help us to continue to provide great books, and it will help our potential buyers make confident buying decisions. Thank you in advance!

REFERENCES

A., A. (2021, August 19). *What is psychological inertia? or... What is wrong with us?* PRIZ Guru. https://www.priz.guru/what-is-psychological-inertia-or-what-is-wrong-with-us/

Aristotle. (n.d.). *Aristotle quote.* Goodreads. https://www.goodreads.com/quotes/3102-knowing-yourself-is-the-beginning-of-all-wisdom

Arundel, K. (2022, December 14). *Survey: Most high school graduates don't feel prepared for college, career decisions.* K-12 Dive. https://www.k12dive.com/news/high-school-graduates-unprepared-for-college-career-decisions/638769/

Asenov, E. (2022, September 8). *Resume for a 16-year-old.* Enhancv. https://enhancv.com/blog/resume-for-a-16-year-old/

Barry. (2018, October 22). *"Documenting little details of your everyday life becomes a celebration of who you are."* The Quotable Coach. https://www.thequotablecoach.com/documenting-details-of-everyday-life/

Bernacki, E. (2023, August 25). *How to be an active participant at conference workshops and breakouts.* Medium. https://ed-bernacki.medium.com/how-to-be-an-active-participant-at-conference-workshops-and-breakouts-99809a234035

Berzman, R. (2023, June3). *How to balance work while going to school (specific tips).* Indeed. https://www.indeed.com/career-advice/career-development/how-to-balance-work-and-school

Bhalla, A. (2024). *I always flew high to laugh loud: When I fall, I stand tall.* Notion Press.

Big five trait: Openness. (n.d.). Crystal. https://www.crystalknows.com/big-five/openness#:~:text=The%20Openness%20trait%20assesses%20how

Birt, J. (2024, April 9). *How to use the STAR interview response technique.* Indeed. https://www.indeed.com/career-advice/interviewing/how-to-use-the-star-interview-response-technique

Boogaard, K. (2020, June 19). *5 career-boosting reasons you should volunteer (in addition to the fact that it makes you a good person).* The Muse. https://www.themuse.com/advice/5-careerboosting-reasons-you-should-volunteer-in-addition-to-the-fact-that-it-makes-you-a-good-person

Bothra, K. (2023, September 11). *Importance of a good resume.* LinkedIn. https://www.linkedin.com/pulse/importance-good-resume-kalp-bothra/

Bradford, C. (n.d.). CHRIS BRADFORD QUOTE. A-Z Quotes. https://www.azquotes.com/quote/522566

Bright, A. (2023, November 7). *33 questions to ask your mentor.* Chronus. https://chronus.com/blog/questions-to-ask-your-mentor?__lai_s=0.0033333333333333333&__lai_sr=0-4&__lai_sl=l

Career clusters and career pathways. (n.d.). ASVAB Career Exploration Program. Asvabprogram.com. https://www.asvabprogram.com/career-cluster

Career clusters and pathways - how to choose. (n.d.). Career Key. https://www.careerkey.org/fit/clusters-pathways/career-clusters-and-career-pathways

Cassell, W. (2022, November 29). *Who is Martha Stewart?* Investopedia. https://www.investopedia.com/articles/professionals/071415/how-martha-stewart-built-media-empire.asp#:~:text=Down%20from%20over%20a%20billion

Chang, L. (2006). *Wisdom for the soul: Five millennia of prescriptions for spiritual healing.* Gnosophia Publishers.

Cherry, K. (2023, March 28). *How to achieve flow.* Verywell Mind. https://www.verywellmind.com/what-is-flow-2794768#toc-how-to-achieve-flow

Cherry, K. (2023a, November 13). *Why learning more about your personality type can benefit your life.* Verywell Mind.

https://www.verywellmind.com/reasons-to-learn-more-about-your-personality-type-4099388#toc-benefits-of-personality-tests

Culver, A. (August 2). *Here's how to find summer jobs for teens*. Snagajob. https://www.snagajob.com/blog/post/teen-summer-jobs

Cuncic, A. (2024, February 12). *7 Active listening techniques for better communication*. Verywell Mind. https://www.verywellmind.com/what-is-active-listening-3024343

Davis, T. (2023, December 3). *Emotional intelligence and how to increase it*. Psychology Today. https://www.psychologytoday.com/za/blog/click-here-for-happiness/202011/emotional-intelligence-and-how-to-increase-it

Debara, D. (2022, September 26). *What is company culture and how do you develop it?* Better Up. https://www.betterup.com/blog/what-is-company-culture

Depaty, L. (n.d.). *The importance of internships for high school students*. EF Academy Blog. https://www.ef.com/wwen/blog/efacademyblog/importance-internships/

DoSomething Editors. (2022, March 15). *8 volunteer opportunities for teens in 2020*. DoSomething. https://www.dosomething.org/us/articles/volunteer-opportunities-for-teens

Doyle, A. (2024, May 3). *How to create an elevator pitch (with examples)*. The Balance. https://www.thebalancemoney.com/elevator-speech-examples-and-writing-tips-2061976#toc-when-and-how-to-use-an-elevator-pitch-or-speech

Duermyer, R. (2020, May 27). *A freelancer's guide to the gig economy*. The Balance. https://www.thebalancemoney.com/what-is-freelancing-1794415#toc-the-advantages-of-freelancing

Easy-to-use one-page business plan template. (2022, March 16). Monday Blog. https://monday.com/blog/project-management/one-page-business-plan/

Einstein, A. (n.d.). *Albert Einstein quote*. BrainyQuote. https://www.brainyquote.com/quotes/albert_einstein_148778

11 ways volunteering can help you find a job. (n.d.). Alberta Alis. https://alis.alberta.ca/look-for-work/work-options/11-ways-volunteering-can-help-you-find-a-job/#:~:text=Your%20volunteer%20experience%20shows%20that

Evans, S. (2023, September 13). *Is college worth it? The pros and cons of college.* Educations.com. https://www.educations.com/articles-and-advice/is-college-worth-it-23605

Fall, K. (2022, January 4). *The meaning of mentorship.* LinkedIn. https://www.linkedin.com/pulse/meaning-mentorship-kathy-fall/

Fisher, A. (2016, June 28). *Here's why you should put volunteer work on your resume.* Fortune. https://fortune.com/2016/06/28/volunteer-work-resume/

F1 Hire. (2024, April 26). *Intern series: From intern to employee: Navigating the transition successfully.* LinkedIn. https://www.linkedin.com/pulse/intern-series-from-employee-navigating-transition-successfully-auafe/

Forsey, C. (2024, April 10). *How to develop a content strategy: A start-to-finish guide.* Hubspot. https://blog.hubspot.com/marketing/content-marketing-plan

Franklin, B. (n.d.). BENJAMIN FRANKLIN QUOTE. BrainyQuote. https://www.brainyquote.com/quotes/benjamin_franklin_138217

Frasier, A. (2016). *Don't dumb down your greatness: A young entrepreneur's guide to thinking & being great.* Anthony Frasier.

Giang, V. (2014, January 3). *It takes just 3 seconds to make a brilliant first impression.* Business Insider. https://www.businessinsider.com/how-to-make-a-great-first-impression-2014-1

Gig economy statistics 2024: Demographics and trends. (2024). TeamStage. https://teamstage.io/gig-economy-statistics/#:~:text=How%20many%20Americans%20are%20in

Githumbi, N. (2023, August 30). *Navigating the digital landscape: Modern strategies for effective job searching.* LinkedIn. https://www.linkedin.com/pulse/navigating-digital-landscape-modern-strategies-job-nancy-githumbi/

Gookin, J. (2002). *Wilderness wisdom: Quotes for inspirational exploration.* Stackpole Books.

Gottsegen, M. (2023, November 22). *Navigating legal requirements for your side hustle: A comprehensive guide.* Medium. https://medium.com/@hk590984/navigating-legal-requirements-for-your-side-hustle-a-comprehensive-guide-1e097ffafeb4

Green, A. (2023, July 25). *How to write a cover letter that will get you a job.* The Cut. https://www.thecut.com/article/how-to-write-a-cover-letter.html

Harris, S. (2020, May 1). *The benefits of automation in today's workforce.* Forbes. https://www.forbes.com/sites/forbestechcouncil/2020/05/01/the-benefits-of-automation-in-todays-workforce/?sh=354ab1021cc8

Herrity, J. (2023, February 17). *The pros and cons of working from home.* Indeed. https://www.indeed.com/career-advice/finding-a-job/the-pros-and-cons-of-working-from-home

Herrity, J. (2023, July 8). *How to tailor your resume to a job description (with example).* Indeed. https://www.indeed.com/career-advice/resumes-cover-letters/tailoring-resume

Herrity, J. (2024a, February 1). *6 qualities that make a great team player.* Indeed, https://www.indeed.com/career-advice/career-development/team-player-qualities

Herrity, J. (2024b, April 9). *How to write a cover letter (with tips and examples).* Indeed. https://www.indeed.com/career-advice/resumes-cover-letters/how-to-write-a-cover-letter

How and why teens should discover their passion. (2016, February 22). Middle Earth. https://middleearthnj.org/2016/02/22/how-and-why-teens-should-discover-their-passion/

How can you use the Socratic method to help clients solve problems? (n.d.). LinkedIn. https://www.linkedin.com/advice/3/how-can-you-use-socratic-method-help-clients

How do you make your online profile work for you? (n.d.). LinkedIn. https://www.linkedin.com/advice/3/how-do-you-make-your-online-profile-work

How to foster a growth mindset in the classroom. (2020, December 10). American University. https://soeonline.american.edu/blog/growth-mindset-in-the-classroom/

Hurley, K. (2024, February 17). *What is resilience? Your guide to facing life's challenges, adversities, and crises.* Everyday Health. https://www.everydayhealth.com/wellness/resilience/

The importance of aligning your personal values with work. (n.d.). HOST. https://wearehostcommunity.com/articles/the-importance-of-aligning-your-personal-values-with-work

Impraim, L. (2017, November 13). *Seeing rejection as redirection: What we gain when we lose.* Tiny Buddha. https://tinybuddha.com/blog/seeing-rejection-as-redirection-what-we-gain-when-we-lose/

Indeed Editorial Team. (2022, June 25). *Career values: How to identify yours and cultivate success as a professional.* Indeed. https://www.indeed.com/career-advice/career-development/career-values

Indeed Editorial Team. (2023, March 10). *How to find a mentor: a useful step-by-step guide.* Indeed. https://uk.indeed.com/career-advice/career-development/how-to-a-find-mentor

Indeed Editorial Team. (2023, March 12). *How to discover: "What am I good at?" (with tips).* Indeed. https://ca.indeed.com/career-advice/finding-a-job/what-am-i-good-at

Indeed Editorial Team. (2023, April 28). *How many applications does it take to get a job? (with FAQs).* Indeed. https://uk.indeed.com/career-advice/finding-a-job/how-many-applications-to-get-job#:~:text=Aiming%20for%20somewhere%20between%2010,of%20coverage%20for%20job%20opportunities.

Jank, H. (2020). Know then thyself. LifeRich Publishing.

Jason. (2023, August 31). *How to get an internship in high school: A step-by-step guide.* Campus to Career Crossroads. https://campustocareercrossroads.com/get-an-internship-in-high-school/

Jociute, D. (2024, January 2). *What is the lean startup methodology?* Viima. https://www.viima.com/blog/lean-startup

Johnson, B. (2023, February 16). *39 famous "failures" to inspire success.* LinkedIn. https://www.linkedin.com/pulse/39-famous-failures-inspire-success-broden-johnson/

Kay, R. (n.d.). *Research the Side Hustle Market!* Refer.io. https://refer.io/blog/articles/research-the-side-hustle-market

Keenan, M. (2024, March 8). *How to do market research: Types and templates (2024).* Shopify. https://www.shopify.com/za/blog/what-is-market-research

Kenton, W. (2022, December 23). *Lean startup: Defined, how it differs from a traditional business.* Investopedia. https://www.investopedia.com/terms/l/lean-startup.asp

Khalid, S. (2022, October 31). *What is self-branding? Why is it important for business.* LinkedIn. https://www.linkedin.com/pulse/what-self-branding-why-important-business-salman-khalid/

Kiersz, A. (2019, October 10). *20 jobs popular in the 1950s that are almost gone today.* Business Insider. https://www.businessinsider.com/jobs-popular-in-the-1950s-that-have-almost-disappeared

Krawcheck, S. (n.d.). Quote. In *Sallie Krawcheck reveals the #1 unwritten rule of success.* (2013, September 17). The Huffington Post. https://www.huffpost.com/entry/sallie-krawcheck_n_3937342

Krawczyk, B. (2023, June 21). *Type 1 vs. type 2 decisions: The art of decision-making in business.* LogRocket Blog. https://blog.logrocket.com/product-management/type-1-vs-type-2-decisions-overview-examples/

Kurtuy, A. (2024, April 12). *How to write a cover letter [full guide & examples for 2024].* Novoresume. https://novoresume.com/career-blog/how-to-write-a-cover-letter-guide

Ladders Inc. (2018, November 6). *Ladders updates popular recruiter eye-tracking study with new key insights on how job seekers can improve their resumes.* PR Newswire. https://www.prnewswire.com/news-releases/ladders-updates-popular-recruiter-eye-tracking-study-with-new-key-insights-on-how-job-seekers-can-improve-their-resumes-300744217.html

Laskowski, N., & Tucci, L. (2022, July 1). *What is artificial intelligence (AI)? Everything you need to know.* TechTarget. https://www.techtarget.com/searchenterpriseai/definition/AI-Artificial-Intelligence

LeBlanc, D., & Howard, M. (2002). *Writing secure code.* Pearson Education.

Levine, A. G. (2020, May 4). *How to handle rejection in your professional life.* Science. https://www.science.org/content/article/how-handle-rejection-your-professional-life

Macready, H. (2024, February 15). *51 LinkedIn statistics you need to know in 2024.* Hootsuite Social Media Management. https://blog.hootsuite.com/linkedin-statistics-business/

Marketiff. (2023, December 15). *Tips to balance your schedule between college and your side hustles.* Harrington Housing. https://www.harringtonhousing.com/news/tips-to-balance-your-schedule-between-college-and-your-side-hustles

Marlin, D. (2017, April 21). *27 quotes to change how you think about problems.* Entrepreneur. https://www.entrepreneur.com/leadership/27-quotes-to-change-how-you-think-about-problems/288957

McKay, D. O. (n.d.). *David O. McKay quote.* BrainyQuote. https://www.brainyquote.com/quotes/david_o_mckay_142152

Menjivar, J. (n.d.). *The ultimate guide to volunteering for teens.* DoSomething. https://www.dosomething.org/us/articles/the-ultimate-guide-to-volunteering-for-teens

Michail, J. (2020, August 24). *Strong nonverbal skills matter now more than ever in this "New normal."* Forbes. https://www.forbes.com/sites/forbescoachescouncil/2020/08/24/strong-nonverbal-skills-matter-now-more-than-ever-in-this-new-normal/?sh=1efa354d5c61

Millington, A. (2018, July 31). *J.K. Rowling's pitch for "Harry Potter" was rejected 12 times — read the now-famous letter here.* Business Insider. https://www.businessinsider.com/revealed-jk-rowlings-original-pitch-for-harry-potter-2017-10

Mind Tools Content Team. (n.d.). *Crafting an elevator pitch.* Mind Tools. https://www.mindtools.com/aofwxxv/crafting-an-elevator-pitch

Mind Tools Content Team. (2022). *Body language.* Mind Tools. https://www.mindtools.com/aejjzul/body-language

Mind Tools Content Team. (2023). *Developing resilience.* Mind Tools. https://www.mindtools.com/ao310a2/developing-resilience

Minimum Viable Product (MVP). (2017, June 27). Agile Alliance. https://www.agilealliance.org/glossary/mvp/

Mintz, S. (2018, August 8). *What are values?* Ethics Sage. https://www.ethicssage.com/2018/08/what-are-values.html

Modi, P. (2023, September 8). *Empowering teens to find their passion: Expert guidance and tips.* Education Next. https://www.educationnext.in/posts/empowering-teens-to-find-their-passion-expert-guidance-and-tips

Nafte, D. (2017, September 10). *Colonel Sanders failed 1009 times before succeeding.* Medium. https://medium.com/@dennisnafte/colonel-sanders-failed-1009-times-before-succeeding-ac5492a5c191

Nguyen, A. (2019, July 3). *Three practical steps to truly uncover your natural talents.* Forbes. https://www.forbes.com/sites/forbescoachescouncil/2019/07/03/three-practical-steps-to-truly-uncover-your-natural-talents/?sh=21f069e51082

Nimbalkar, M. (2023, May 16). *Establishing a successful mentor-mentee relationship: Initiating the first meeting.* LinkedIn. https://www.linkedin.com/pulse/establishing-successful-mentor-mentee-relationship-first-nimbalkar/

Nyst, A. (2023, October 27). *Social media branding: How to get it right.* Search Engine Journal. https://www.searchenginejournal.com/social-media-branding/496753/

Ogunbona, P. (2019, July 31). *How To Find Your Passion and Become a Successful Entrepreneur.* LinkedIn. https://www.linkedin.com/pulse/how-find-your-passion-become-successful-entrepreneur-ogunbona/

Our company. (n.d.). Indeed. https://uk.indeed.com/about/our-company

Ovalekar, M. (2021, March 19). *Importance of internships for high-school students.* Global Career Counsellor Certification. https://www.globalcareercounsellor.com/blog/importance-of-internships-for-high-school-students/

Parker, K. (2023, March 30). *About a third of U.S. workers who can work from home now do so all the time.* Pew Research Center. https://www.pewresearch.org/short-reads/2023/03/30/about-a-third-of-us-workers-who-can-work-from-home-do-so-all-the-time/

Pavlou, C. (2019, July 16). *Hard skills vs. soft skills.* Recruiting resources: How to recruit and hire better. Workable. https://resources.workable.com/hr-terms/hard-skills-vs-soft-skills#h21

Peale, N. V. (2023). *The power of positive thinking.* Bibliomania Publishing & Distribution Cairo, Egypt.

Perry, E. (2023, July 25). *20 personal values examples to help you find your own.* BetterUp. https://www.betterup.com/blog/personal-values-examples

Persona. (2023, November 6). *Strategic networking: How to craft a career plan in 7 steps.* Persona. Https://Www.personatalent.com. https://www.personatalent.com/leadership/strategic-networking

Platts, K., Breckon, J., & Marshall, E. (2022). Enforced home-working under lockdown and its impact on employee wellbeing: a cross-sectional study. *BMC Public Health, 22*(1). https://doi.org/10.1186/s12889-022-12630-1

Pratt, E. (2024, February 2). *When someone has a fear of the unknown.* Verywell Health. https://www.verywellhealth.com/fear-of-the-unknown-5208919#toc-treatment

Proe, P. (2017, November 27). *How to find your passion in life (and not just for college admissions).* Your Teen Magazine. https://yourteenmag.com/teenager-school/teens-high-school/how-to-find-your-passion-in-life

Rainie, L., Funk, C., Anderson, M., & Tyson, A. (2022, March 17). *AI and human enhancement: Americans' openness is tempered by a range of concerns.* Pew Research Center.

https://www.pewresearch.org/internet/2022/03/17/ai-and-human-enhancement-americans-openness-is-tempered-by-a-range-of-concerns/

Resilience: Building resilience: Overcoming challenges through change. (2024, April 17). FasterCapital. https://fastercapital.com/content/Resilience--Building-Resilience--Overcoming-Challenges-through-Change.html

Revesencio, J. (2015, July 22). *Why happy employees are 12% more productive.* Fast Company. https://www.fastcompany.com/3048751/happy-employees-are-12-more-productive-at-work

Romano, C. (2023, July 18). *10 ways to identify your talents and utilize them.* Lifehack. https://www.lifehack.org/articles/productivity/10-ways-identify-your-talents-and-utilize-them.html

Romano, J. (2015, June 30). *21 inspirational career quotes.* Linkedin, https://www.linkedin.com/pulse/21-inspirational-career-quotes-judy-romano-mba/

Rose, R. (2023, February 25). *Questions to ask yourself after failure.* Your Perfect Dreams. https://www.yourperfectdreams.com/questions-to-ask-yourself-after-failure/

Rouse, M. (2023, June 26). *Automation.* Techopedia. https://www.techopedia.com/definition/32099/automation

Runyan, A. (2012, August 21). *How to envision a great future career for yourself.* Classy Career Girl. https://www.classycareergirl.com/how-to-envision-a-great-future-career-for-yourself/

Ryan, E. (2024, March 22). *Growth mindset vs fixed mindset: What do they really mean?* Mentorloop Mentoring Software. https://mentorloop.com/blog/growth-mindset-vs-fixed-mindset-what-do-they-really-mean/

Segal, J., Smith, M., Robinson, L., & Shubin, J. (2024, February 5). *Improving emotional intelligence (EQ).* HelpGuide. https://www.helpguide.org/articles/mental-health/emotional-intelligence-eq.htm

Sellas, B. B. (2023, April 7). *How to use social media for professional networking.* LinkedIn. https://www.linkedin.com/pulse/how-use-social-media-professional-networking-brooke-b-sellas/

Shakespeare, W. (n.d.). WILLIAM SHAKESPEARE QUOTE. BrainyQuote. https://www.brainyquote.com/quotes/william_shakespeare_101458

Shopify Staff. (2022, December 10). *What is marketing? Learn 4 principles of marketing.* Shopify. https://www.shopify.com/za/blog/what-is-marketing

Shorelight Team. (2023, July 10). *How to create your career action plan in 4 easy steps.* Shorelight. https://shorelight.com/student-stories/career-action-plan-in-4-steps/

The 6 most common leadership styles & how to find yours. (2024, February). IMD. https://www.imd.org/reflections/leadership-styles/#:~:text=Detailed%20feedback%20is%20one%20easy

Skusa, M. (2022, December 5). *What is a feedback loop? – 6 feedback loop examples.* Filestage. https://filestage.io/blog/feedback-loops/

S., L. (2023, May 12). *Critical thinking & problem-solving - An essential skill at work.* LinkedIn. https://www.linkedin.com/pulse/critical-thinking-problem-solving-essential-skill-work-lata-singh/

SMART goals for career development examples. (2024, January 25). Centier. https://www.centier.com/resources/articles/smart-goals-for-career-development-examples

Smith, A. (n.d.). *7 job search tips everyone should know.* Monster. https://www.monster.com/career-advice/article/job-search-hacks

Storeplum Editorial. (2023, October 31). *100 hustle and grind quotes to get you motivated.* Storeplum. https://www.storeplum.com/blogs/grind-hustle-quotes#inspiring-hustle-quotes

Stuck, A. (2023, March 15). *Fear of the unknown: Causes, signs, & how to overcome.* Choosing Therapy. https://www.choosingtherapy.com/fear-of-the-unknown/

Struyk, T. (2024, March 26). *Top 5 benefits of a summer job—besides pay.* Investopedia. https://www.investopedia.com/financial-edge/0610/top-5-benefits-of-a-summer-job---besides-pay.aspx#toc-what-are-the-top-5-benefits-of-a-summer-job-besides-pay

Sutton, A. (2012). *52 ways to transform your life.* Troubador Publishing Ltd.

Sutton, J. (2023, October 3). *How to create a personal development plan: 3 examples.* Positive Psychology. https://positivepsychology.com/personal-development-plan/#how-to-create-a-personal-development-plan

Tabac, M. (2021, October 11). *The neuroscience of journaling and its benefits.* Medium. https://medium.com/clear-yo-mind/the-neuroscience-of-journaling-and-its-benefits-a91218773159

Taj, K. (2019, April 2). *7 ways to reframe failure.* Medium. https://kam-taj-coaching.medium.com/7-ways-to-reframe-failure-10e9c511f698

Team Everlance. (2022, May 11). *What is a side hustle? [+ how to start one in 4 easy steps!].* Everlance. https://www.everlance.com/blog/side-hustle-meaning

10 things to do right in an interview. (2022, January 7). Iowa Pomerantz Career Center. https://careers.uiowa.edu/careerbuzz/201509/10-things-do-right-interview

Tham, M. (2019, March 11). *Top 5 skills you need to survive the digital age.* Noodle Factory. https://articles.noodlefactory.ai/top-5-skills-you-need-to-survive-the-digital-age

Tips for online communication in the workplace. (n.d.). Aberta Alis. https://alis.alberta.ca/succeed-at-work/make-your-work-life-more-satisfying/tips-for-online-communication-in-the-workplace/

Tips for teenagers on finding that first job. (2022, March 10). The Parents Website. https://theparentswebsite.com.au/tips-for-teenagers-on-finding-that-first-job/

Tips to help your teen cultivate their passion. (2019, December 31). Raising Healthy Teens. https://raisinghealthyteens.org/tips-to-help-your-teen-cultivate-their-passion/

Ulises. (2021, December 17). *10 ways to start finding your passions as a teenager.* Knit Marketing. https://knitmarketing.com/blog/10-ways-to-start-finding-your-passions-as-a-teenager/

Venezia, C. (2023, May 9). *Redefining success with nonlinear career paths*. Forbes. https://www.forbes.com/sites/forbesbusinesscouncil/2023/05/09/redefining-success-with-nonlinear-career-paths/?sh=59941d543f57

Volunteering can build a stronger resume. (2022, January 3). Rio Salado College. https://www.riosalado.edu/news/2022/volunteering-can-build-stronger-resume

Walter, E. (2013, December 30). *30 powerful quotes on failure*. Forbes. https://www.forbes.com/sites/ekaterinawalter/2013/12/30/30-powerful-quotes-on-failure/?sh=47b7be7724bd

What are skills? (n.d.). Lightcast. https://lightcast.io/what-are-skills

What are the best job search strategies for finding conferences and events to attend? (n.d.). LinkedIn. https://www.linkedin.com/advice/1/what-best-job-search-strategies-finding-conferences-lst5f#:~:text=You%20can%20use%20online%20platforms

What is the gig economy? (n.d.). GCFGlobal. https://edu.gcfglobal.org/en/freelance-work/what-is-the-gig-economy/1/

What should I major in? 10 essential questions to ask yourself. (2021, April 29). Worldwide Learn. https://www.worldwidelearn.com/articles/10-questions-for-picking-a-major/

Whitehorn, K. (n.d.). *Katharine Whitehorn quote*. BrainyQuote. https://www.brainyquote.com/quotes/katharine_whitehorn_102412

Wojno, R. (2023, January 1). *6 crucial effective team management tips*. Monday Blog. https://monday.com/blog/teamwork/team-management/

Wyman, N. (2023, June 13). *Unlocking success: Five strategies for maximizing your summer internship experience*. Forbes. https://www.forbes.com/sites/nicholaswyman/2023/06/13/unlocking-success-five-strategies-for-maximizing-your-summer-internship-experience/?sh=732897152a89

Zaidi, A. (2018). *Face time: Event planning for business success*. iUniverse.

Zane, M. (2022, August 23). *What percentage of jobs are found through networking?* Zippia. https://www.zippia.com/advice/what-percentage-of-jobs-are-found-through-networking/

Zhang, L. (2020, June 19). *What is an internship and how do you get one?* The Muse. https://www.themuse.com/advice/what-is-an-internship-definition-advice

Zhang, L. (2023, April 13). *Everything you need to know about answering behavioral interview questions.* The Muse. https://www.themuse.com/advice/behavioral-interview-questions-answers-examples

Image References

All images have been purchased from Creative Market (creativemarket.com). The author has the commercial license to use these images.

Made in the USA
Monee, IL
03 December 2024

71884193R00089